Original publication: "Hudební nauka Klíček 1"
Author: Eva Šašinková, M.M., Ph.D., M.B.A.
Illustrations: Mgr. Kateřina Kovářová
Original graphic design: Lumír Kaděra
Original publisher: Czech Music Edition, Prague, Czech Republic, 2022
Website: www.hudebni-publikace.cz
Copyright: Eva Šašinková, M.M., Ph.D., M.B.A.
Original Czech version ISBN: 978-80-907578-6-8

English adaptation: "Clefi's Music Notebook 1"
Illustrations: Mgr. Kateřina Kovářová
Translation, adaptation, and graphic design: Roman Placzek, D.M.A.
Publisher: BumbleBeeNotes™ Music Publishing, Manlius, NY, USA, 2025
Catalog number: cbbn002-wb-006
Website: www.bumblebeenotes.com
Copyright: BumbleBee Notes™ Inc. Music Corporation
ISBN: 979-8-9919035-5-4

Clefi's Little Crossword Review

Down:

1. G clef.
2. The musical symbols for silence in music.
3. The musical symbol for the soft sound.
4. The meaning of the letter C used instead of its numeric time signature alternative.
6. An example of an ordinary sound in nature.
7. A melodic musical sound.
8. Small sections of musical notation helping organize it.
13. The parts of a musical staff.
17. The short lines helping with the placement of notes outside of the staff.
18. The difference between C and D.
19. F clef.
23 The pulse of a musical piece.

Across:

5. The musical grid used to notate music.
9. The scale built from the primary tone row.
10. The musical symbol for the loud sound.
11. A part of the notes shorter than a whole note.
12. A musical piece past through generations by singing.
14. CDEFGAB.
15. A musical instrument playing rhythmical musical sounds.
16. Parts of notes shorter than a quarter note.
20. Short vertical lines separating measures.
21. Smallest difference between two notes.
22. The sense that helps us identify sounds.
24. The time signature.

Eva Šašinková, M.M., Ph.D., MBA, the author of the series, lives in Prague, Czech Republic, where she concertizes and holds academic positions at the Pilsen Conservatory and Academy of Music in Prague. Since childhood, Eva has dreamed of becoming a music teacher, sharing her passion and experience of love for music, especially with children. She has a deep love for the double bass, her instrument, in which she holds a master's degree. However, Eva also profoundly admires the piano, an instrument that was an inseparable part of her

About the Author

childhood. This admiration is the reason behind the concept of her method, which she based on the keyboard's layout. Eva is convinced that the piano is a unique instrument designed to help explain the fundamentals of music theory, the meaning of tones and melody, and the mission of music. She successfully proves her firm conviction in the practical application of her method. The story of her project started with a children's story that came to life during a trying period in the author's life.

Her passion for teaching children and desire to share her knowledge helped her concentrate on the essentials. During her pedagogical activities, Eva noticed that the materials available to her for the curriculum presentation were not, in her professional opinion, satisfactory. She started to visit music schools in her home country, the Czech Republic, comparing, editing, reworking, and creating. As a result, Eva began to bring worksheets filled with information and fun activities to the music education classes to make students' time learning music theory more engaging, easily accessible, and entertaining. The reactions of the young music students and fellow pedagogues were overwhelmingly positive.

Professor Eva managed to engage children's senses from all angles—drawing, singing, and practical demonstrations on a keyboard—everything children appreciated. On top of that, she had "The Story of a Song, "which kicked off a star career for one little boy, Clefi. He welcomes children in his "Clefi's Little Notebook" and helps them learn more in the four volumes of his "Clefi's Music Notebook." He plays and sings with them in "Clefi's Little Music Education Notebook" (in the translated version integrated into "Clefi's Little Notebook" – editor's note) and "Clefi's Musical Instruments" written for little musicians. Clefi helps them practice their newly acquired knowledge in three workbooks full of fun tasks and exercises. Children play with little Clefi, learn, and get ready for the more dedicated encounter with Lady Music and their chosen instrument in a fun and engaging way. And maybe it will become the love of their lives, their calling, and a hobby, as it happened to the author.

And to the sad faces of those who did not have the luck to learn from the best teachers and publications and did not have the best opportunities, Eva says with her clever little smile: "If you love music and have an open heart, the muse will not ask you how old you are. She will kiss you on the brow when you least expect it. So do not wait and be ready!"

Author's Foreword

Clefi's New Music Education School
is a unified music education method for children, amateur musicians, and music students.

Based on my extensive multi-genre musical performing career, many years of experience teaching children, and my terminal education degree in music theory, I have created a unified music education program for children from an early age to young musicians who choose to study music more seriously. The New Music Education School leans on children's natural perception of music. It offers young musicians and their teachers a unified educational system of fundamental music theory aiming to support musical creativity. Its main goal is to awaken children's musicianship based on creativity and the ability to sing a song, play it on a musical instrument of their choice, and write it down correctly, the sort of musicianship that enables them to use their musical knowledge theoretically and practically.

The first book, Clefi's Little Notebook, is tailored for the youngest musicians. It introduces us to Clefi, a charming little boy who shares his story. Clefi becomes our companion on this musical adventure. In Clefi's Little Notebook, children delve into musical notation, the birth of a song, a musical note, a musical staff, a clef (which inspired Clefi's name), the musical alphabet, and a scale. They learn to read and write notes in the fourth, the middle octave, and practice their new skills through exercises, puzzles, engaging tasks, and songs they play and sing.

Clefi's Music Notebooks 1, 2, 3, and **4** follow Clefi's Little Notebook. These four full-color music textbooks stand out for their unique conceptual design. Each volume is a complete unit and can be used individually.

At the same time, all four volumes are designed as one method, seamlessly following one another, so that the children can acquire a complete knowledge of the fundamentals of music theory in a friendly and engaging way.

Beautiful illustrations and graphic design enhance the unique quality of these lovely publications. All textbooks are suitable for children, amateur musicians, and professional music students.

This music education series explains the fundamentals of music theory quickly and efficiently so that children can understand and practice them while playing musical instruments, singing, and harmonizing. The textbooks aim to develop children's musical abilities, aural skills, perception of tone pitch and duration, and rhythmical and tonal melodic structure.

The idea behind this methodological concept is to make children first listen, then understand, learn, utilize, and create. When born, a baby listens and absorbs speech. When it understands it, it tries to pronounce the first words. A child attempts to understand the connections and context. Only after several years can a child logically think and systematically create. And the same applies to the understanding of music! What would the knowledge of music theory be for if we did not listen to music and didn't use the ingenious system of music theory in practice? However, the same applies both ways. How can we expect to evolve in our music-making if we refuse to learn and explore the mysteries of music, its tonal relations, harmony, and rhythm?

This method will help children fully absorb music and learn essential human and life values through it. We can learn to read and write only if we listen to our parents talk from an early age. Then, we learn the words, pronounce them, and understand their meaning. The same applies to music and how we understand it.

I hope my books will bring you joy and help many young musicians open the door to the beautiful world of music.

Eva

What's Inside:

Similar to "Clefi's Little Notebook," this book presents a collection of enchanting folk songs from the rich Czech folklore tradition, designed for music education. To accurately utilize their intended purpose, each song requires accurate adaptation and translation into English, which would take up more space than these volumes can accommodate without disrupting their intended design. Therefore, we are offering a standalone "Clefi & Notelina's Songbook," featuring all the songs from all nine volumes of Clefi's New Music Education School series, along with accurately and sensibly translated and adapted English lyrics.

Dear friends in music,

We have prepared a new series of four workbooks to accompany you on your musical journey. To make our journey even better, I enlisted the help of my friend, Notelina. Notelina knows many songs and has great ideas. We both love the sea world, which is why our first joint Notebook is filled with sea creatures and their friends, the musical symbol.

In the book's first part, we will review the fundamentals of music with you. A review is always good for building and enhancing your knowledge and skills. With a strong foundation, you will be able to play, sing, and write down a song or melody in any key in no time.

We will take a new look at the musical alphabet, notes, and rests. We will expand our understanding of notes in the fourth and third octaves, strengthen our knowledge of the bass clef, and discover more fun facts about accidentals. We will learn about intervals within the major scale and discover how to create scales with sharps. You will also get to know the major fifth chord, which serves as the foundation for accompanying songs.

Additionally, we will talk about different time signatures, explore dotted notes, practice rhythm, and widen our arsenal of symbols in musical notation. Finally, we will explain what a lowered tone is and how to create major scales with flats. And at the end, we will also share an intriguing story about the mysterious tone "H."

Discovering the secrets and fundamentals of music will be fun and enlightening for you. Understanding these concepts is essential for further developing your talent and skills.

We invite you to embark on a journey into the world of music.

Yours,
Clefi and Notelina

MUSICAL ALPHABET

A **tone** is a musical sound.
A **note** is a musical symbol for a **tone**.

MUSICAL ALPHABET

The **musical alphabet** is used to name tones and notes.
It has seven letters indicating the primary tones: C, D, E, F, G, A, and B.
The primary tones of the musical alphabet make up **the primary tone row**.

PIANO KEYBOARD

The piano keyboard has **white** and **black** keys.
The **longer** and **wider white keys** represent the tones of the musical alphabet and the primary tone row that keeps repeating itself for the length of the keyboard.

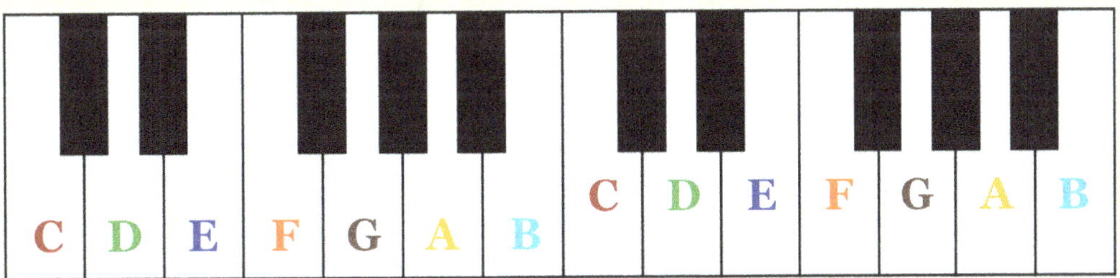

The **shorter** and **narrower black keys** are arranged into two groups: a group of **two keys** and a group of **three keys** with a white key between every black key. The groups are separated by two white keys. This structure helps us in locating the **C** key, which plays note C representing the first tone of the primary tone row.

The **first white key** next to the group of two black keys to the left is **C**, and the white key in between the two black keys is **D**, and so on.

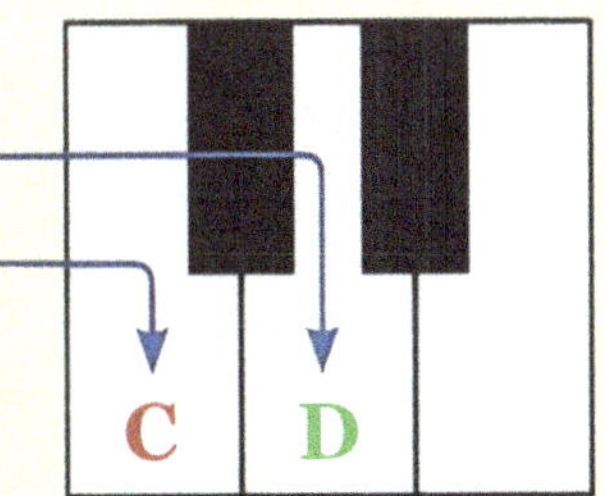

E Write the correct names of the keys into the circles on the keyboard.

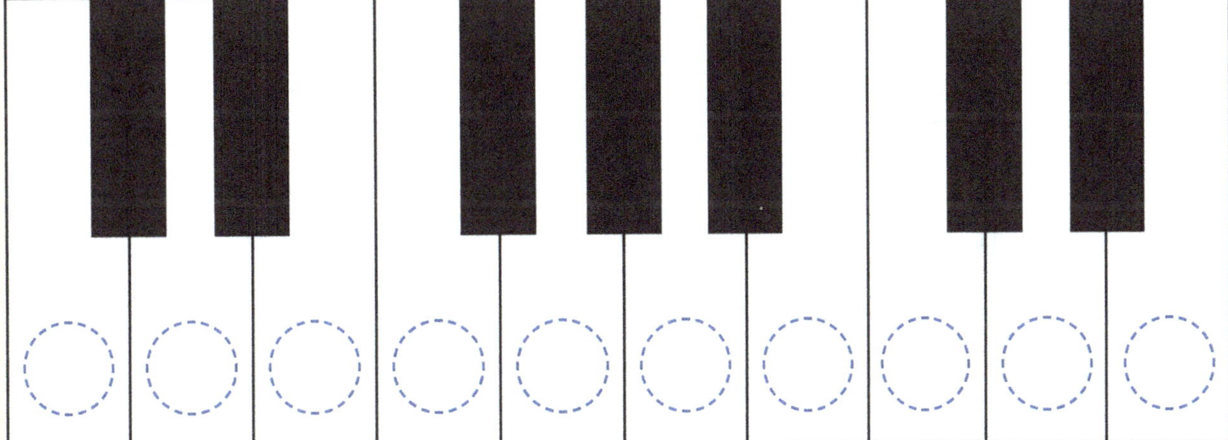

NOTES & RESTS

NOTES

A **note** is **a musical symbol** for **a tone** = musical sound.
Different notes have different looks and counts of beats.

Every note has **a head**, some notes have **a stem**, and some have
a stem with a flag or, when connected, **a beam**.
The look of a note tells us its **length**.

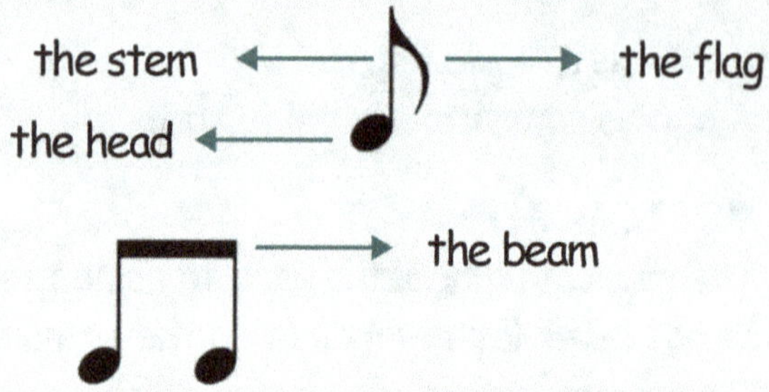

Fundamental Types of Notes

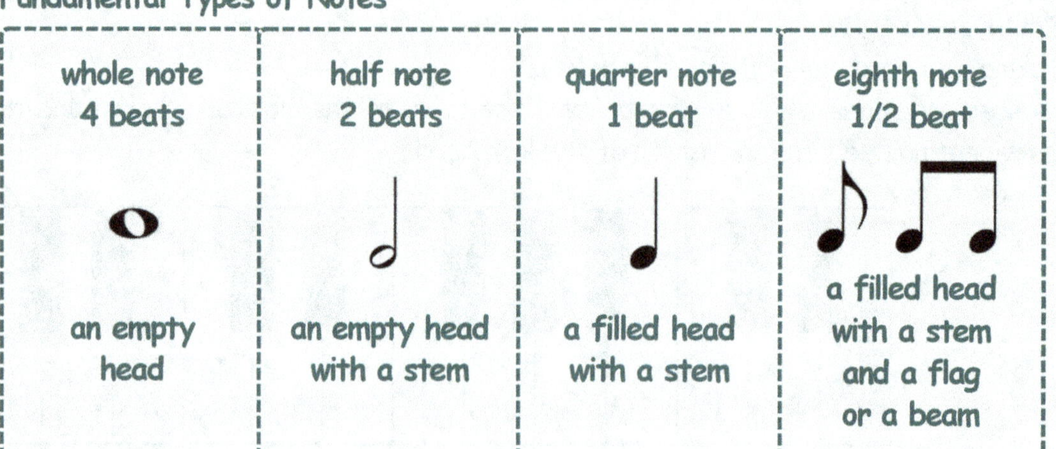

whole note 4 beats	half note 2 beats	quarter note 1 beat	eighth note 1/2 beat
an empty head	an empty head with a stem	a filled head with a stem	a filled head with a stem and a flag or a beam

RESTS

A **rest** is a musical sign for **silence in music**. The looks of different rests and, in the case of the whole and half rests, their placement tell us how long the silence is.

Fundamental Types of Rests

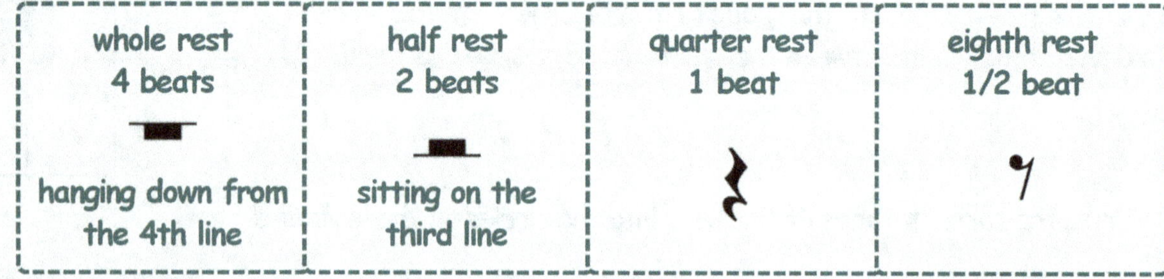

whole rest 4 beats	half rest 2 beats	quarter rest 1 beat	eighth rest 1/2 beat
hanging down from the 4th line	sitting on the third line		

E Copy the notes and rests into empty measures, then write their names in the spaces below.

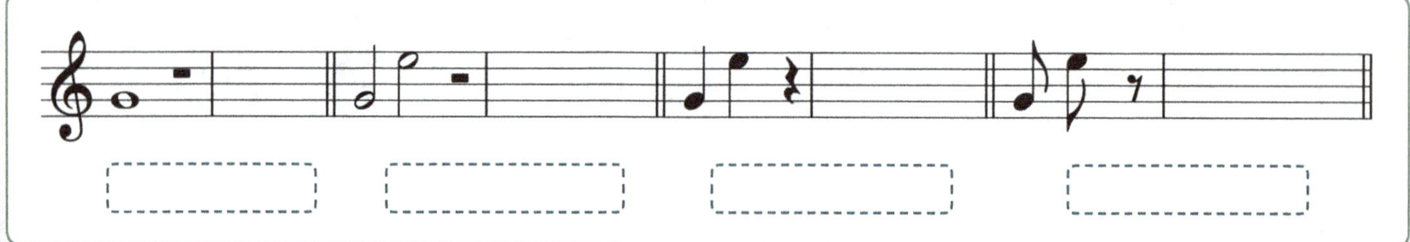

MUSICAL NOTATION

If we want to notate music, we must know the following terms and their definitions: a note, a rest, a musical staff, a clef, a measure, a bar line, and the time signature or meter.

The MUSICAL STAFF has five lines and four spaces that we number from the bottom up. When drawing the notes on the staff, we place them on the lines or in the spaces. If a note sits above the fifth or below the first lines, we use the ledger lines. The ledger lines are short lines, each assigned to a specific note.

The clef is a musical symbol at the begining of the staff. A clef and the placement of the note on the staff determine the pitch of the tone. The most frequently used clef is the treble clef.

Measures are small sections of the musical piece separated by measure lines.
The measure or bar lines are vertical lines on the staff, separating the individual measure.
The time signature or meter tells us the number of beats in one measure and the note value of each beat. We draw it at the beginning of a piece, right after the clef.

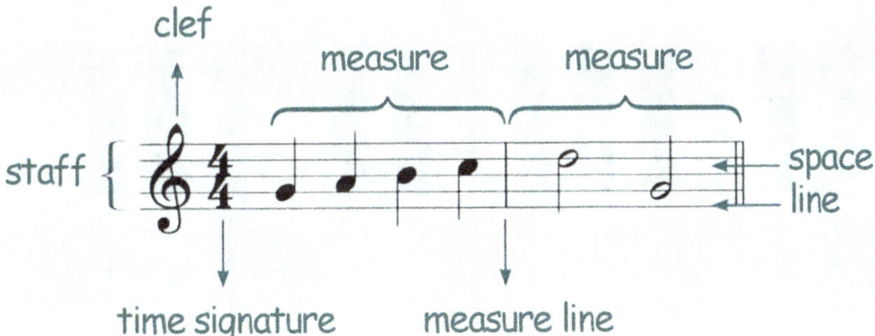

Notes on the Staff
The direction of the note stems is:
- **upward** when the note is in the lower part of the staff
- **downward** when the note is in the upper part of the staff.

The flag starts at the tip of the stem and is always to the right.

E 1. Trace the lines of the staff in red and fill the spaces in yellow.
2. Circle the clef in red and the meter in green, and trace the measure lines in blue.
3. Add the stems to the half notes on the correct side and in the proper direction.

OCTAVES

The primary tone row has **seven** different tones: **C, D, E, F, G, A,** and **B,** which keep repeating at different heights. To organize them better, we stack them up into octaves. Each octave starts with the tone **C**.

The full piano keyboard fits seven full octaves of the primary tones with a couple of tones below the first one on its left side.

E Look at the piano keyboard to see all the octaves and extra keys below the first C, the **C1**.

The octave in the middle of the keyboard is the **MIDDLE OCTAVE**. This octave is number 4 because it is the fourth octave from the left side of the keyboard. The first octave from the left has the number 1, the next one is 2, then 3, and the middle one is the fourth one. It's followed by 5 and 6, and the highest octave is 7.

E Fill in the missing complete names of the notes. Write the number of the octaves into the spaces below.

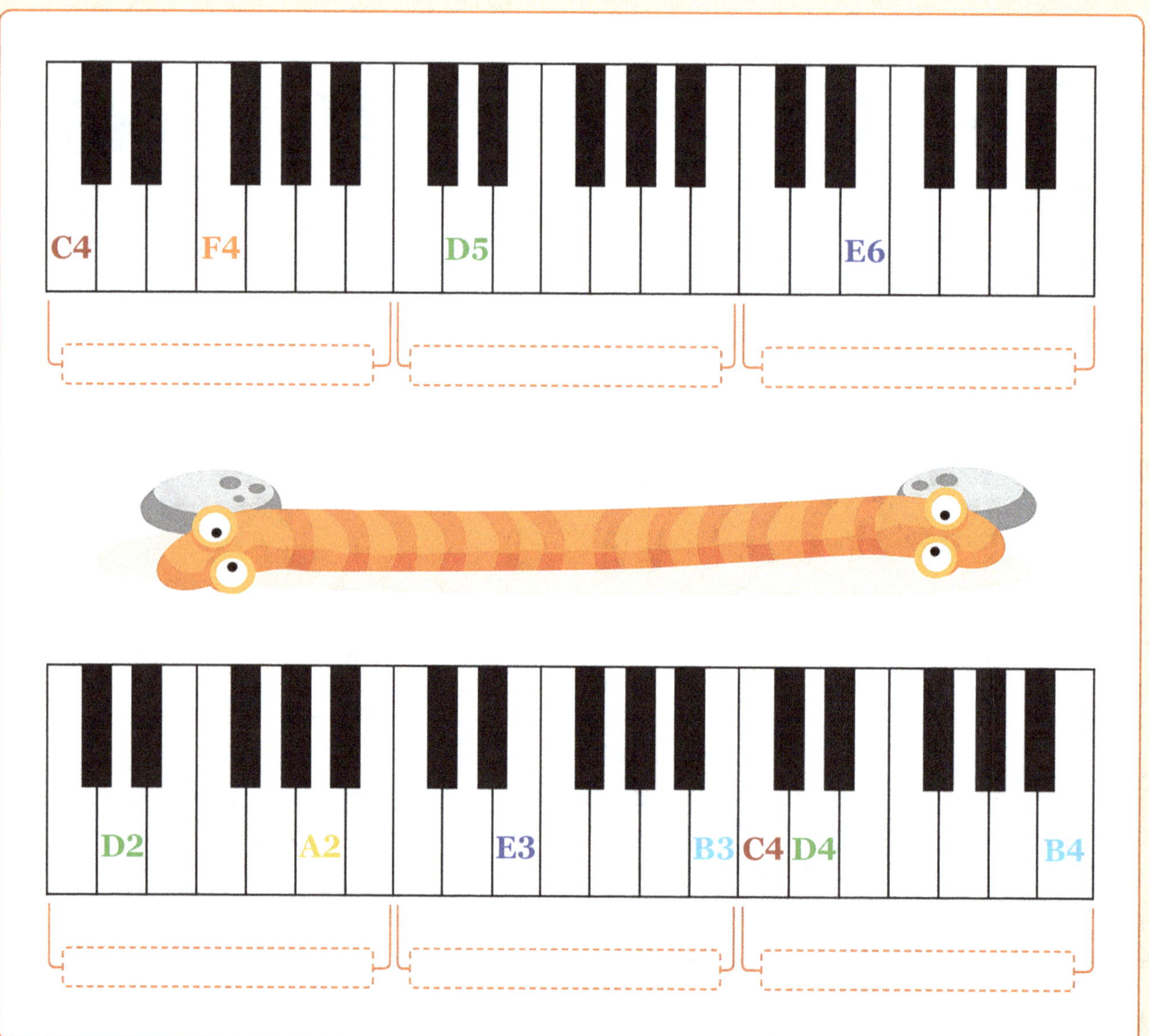

TREBLE CLEF, NOTES C4 - C6

The clef allows us to identify the position and pitch of a note on the staff. Each clef features a reference tone that assists us in recognizing all other tones within the staff. This reference tone also provides the clef with its alternate name.

The treble clef serves to notate high-pitched sounds.
Its reference tone is G4, which is located on the second line of the staff.
Therefore, the treble clef is often referred to as the G clef.

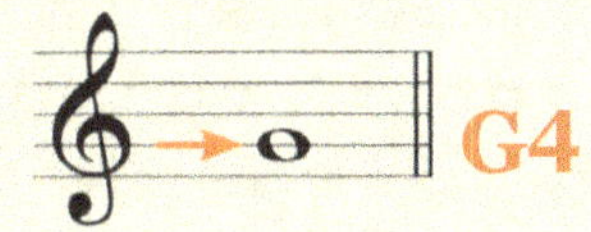

When writing notes on a staff, we follow the same structured approach, moving up or down in accordance with the octaves on the keyboard.

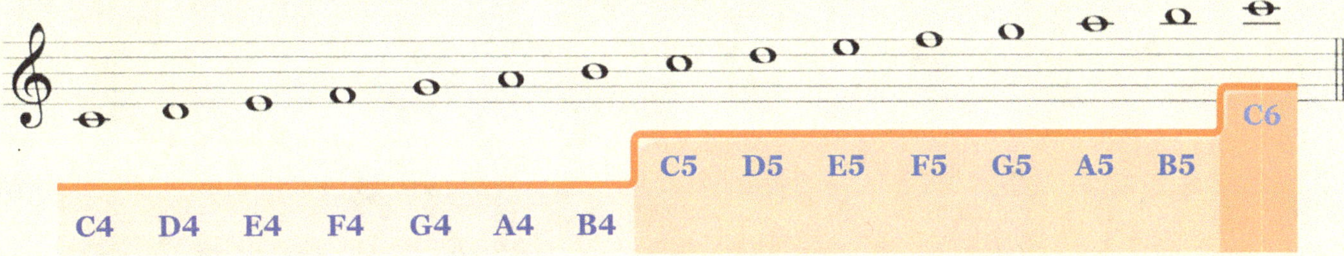

To quickly identify the notes written in the treble clef, we use **the hint word FACE**.
F4, A4, C5, and E5 are the notes that we find in **the spaces of the staff** from the bottom up.

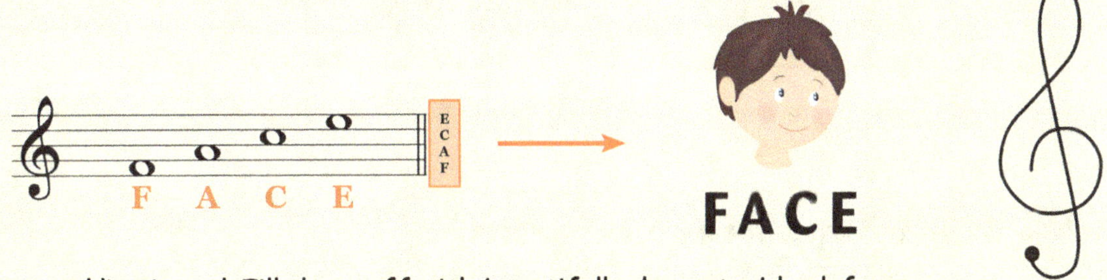

E Trace the second line in red. Fill the staff with beautifully drawn treble clefs.

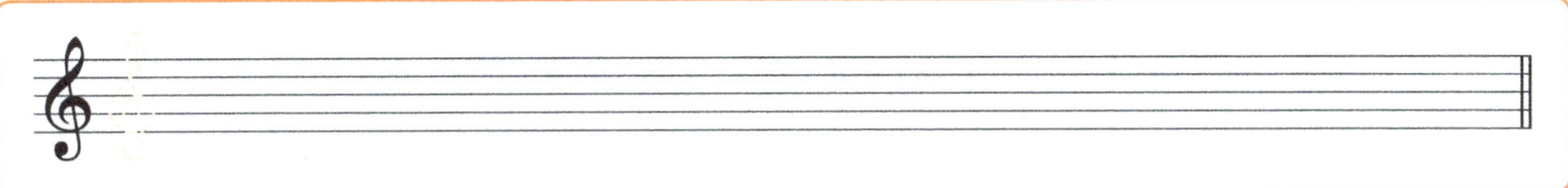

E Write the complete names of the notes in the squares below them.

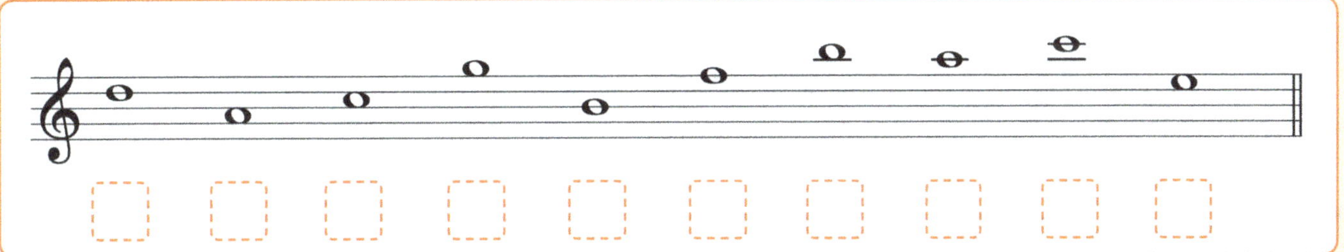

BASS CLEF

If we want to write and read the notes in all octaves and use the full keyboard, we need to know at least two clefs: the treble clef and the bass clef.

The bass clef is used to notate the **low-pitched tones**.
Its reference tone is **F3** on the fourth line of the staff.
The bass clef is also called the F clef.

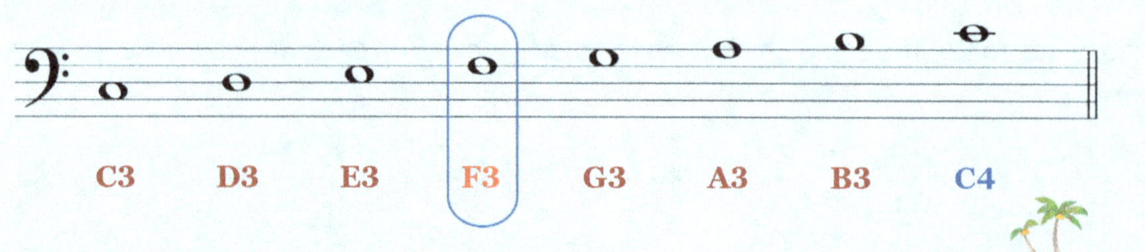

The bass clef starts on the line where the F3 sits.
To make sure that it's clear, we mark it with two dots in the third and fourth lines right after the clef.

E Trace the fourth line in red. Fill the staff with beautifully drawn bass clefs.

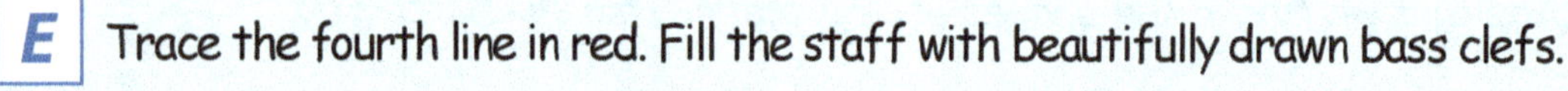

E Draw half notes according to the names below the staff

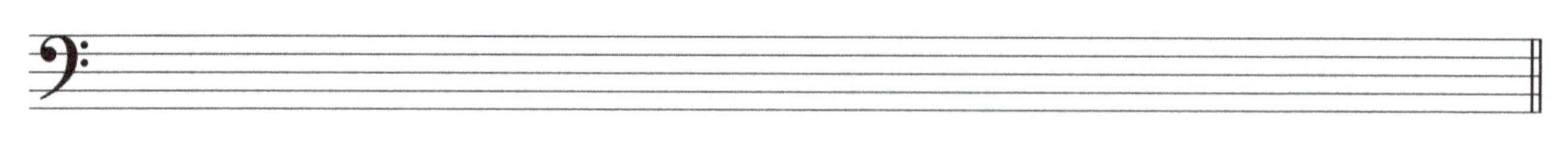

E In the notation, we can see the clef change from the bass to the treble clef.
Write the names of the notes in the squares below the staff.

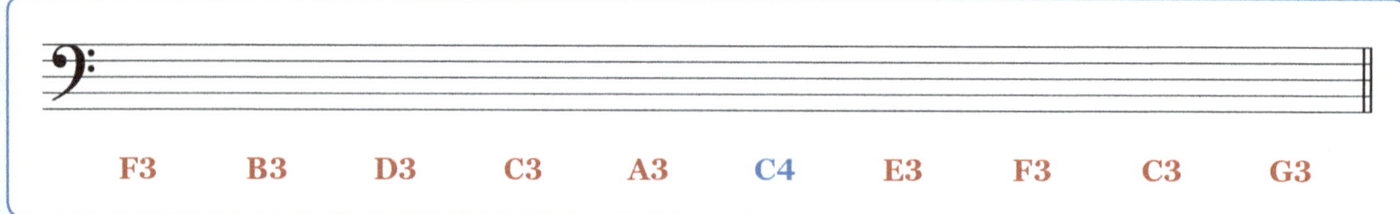

NOTES IN TREBLE & BASS CLEFS

In the **treble clef**, the note *C4* sits
on the first ledger line **below** the staff.

In the **bass clef**, the same note, *C4,* sits
on the first ledger line **above** the staff.

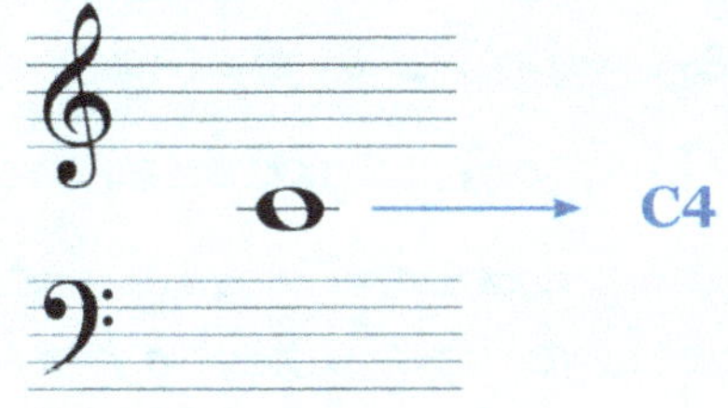

E Some tones are commonly marked in either of the clefs, especially tones **G3 - E4**.
Write the names of the notes into the circles on the keyboard.

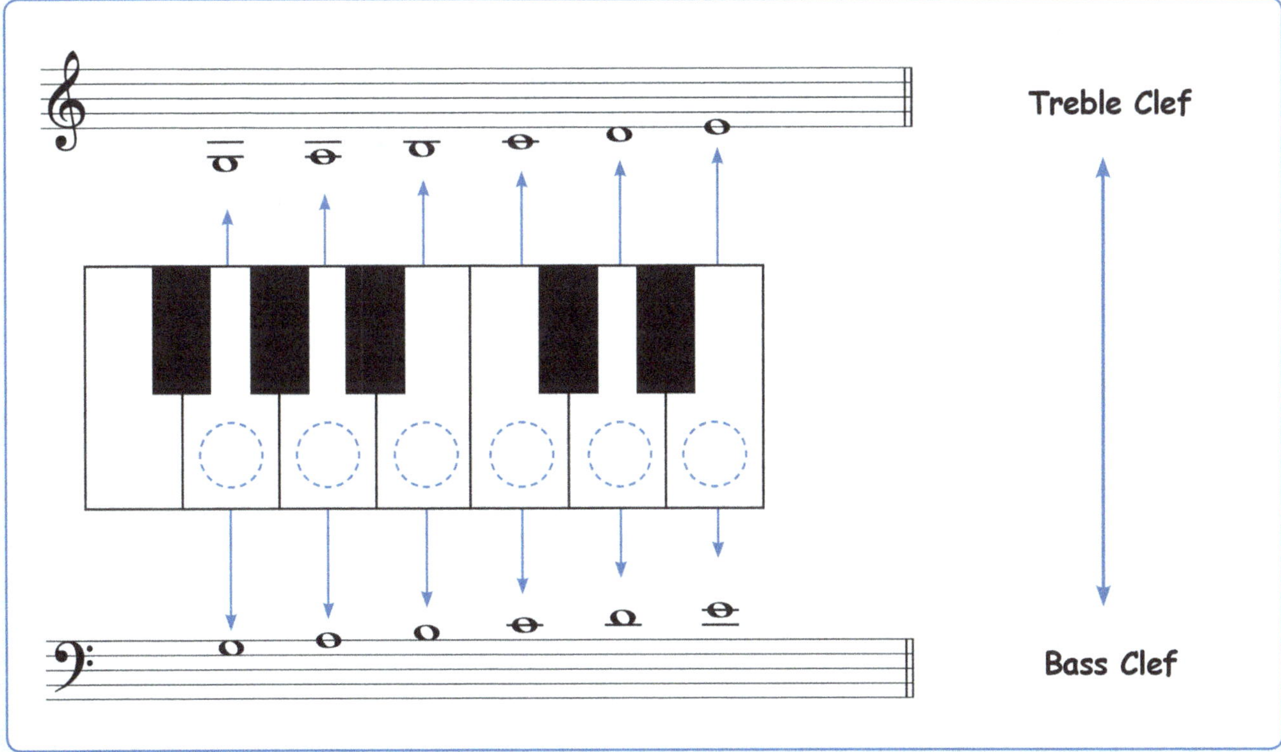

E Look at the section from the song about the bass behind the stove. Write the names of the notes on
the lines, and then draw the same notes in the lower staff in the bass clef.

HALF & WHOLE STEPS

A **HALF STEP** is the smallest distance between two tones. On the keyboard, it's the two immediately neighboring keys regardless of whether they are both white or one is white and the other is black.

A **WHOLE STEP** is the combined distance of two adjacent half steps.

The tones of the fundamental tone row are **whole steps** and **half steps** apart.
Two neighboring white keys **without a black key** between them are **a half step** apart.
Two neighboring white keys **with a black key** between them are **a whole step** apart.

E In the squares below the keyboard, write 1/2 or 1, indicating the half step or whole step between two tones marked with the arrows.

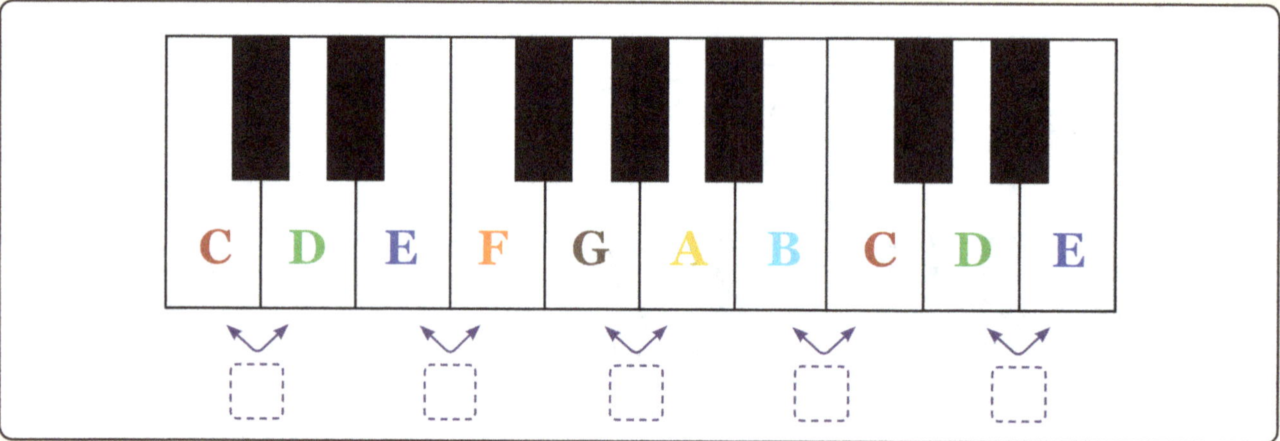

E Show the two notes on the keyboard and write 1/2 or 1 indicating the half step or whole step distance between them.

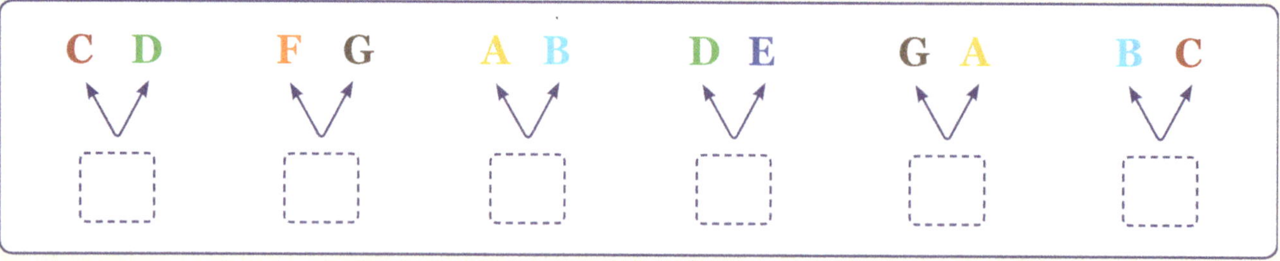

Let's learn to recognize the half-step and whole step by ear. We will use the *Half-step Song* and two folk songs as help. *I Like Grass* (Clefi's Little Notebook pg. 58) starts with an ascending half step, and *A Cat is Coming Down* (Clefi's Little Notebook pg. 54) with a descending whole step.

C MAJOR SCALE

A **SCALE** is a **tone row** organized according to **preset rules**.

The tones C, D, E, F, G, A, B, and C make up the tone row we call a **MAJOR SCALE**. Because this particular scale starts and ends with the tone C, we call it the **C Major** scale.

The **C Major** scale is the **primary major scale**.
It's composed of the tones of the musical alphabet. All its tones are played on the white keys.

In the same way as the tones of the C major scale line up on the keyboard, we write its notes on the staff in a row up, step by step. In the treble clef, the note C4 sits on the first ledger line below the staff. The following notes line up in a row, always one place higher, alternating between the lines and spaces.

E Fill in the full names of the notes.

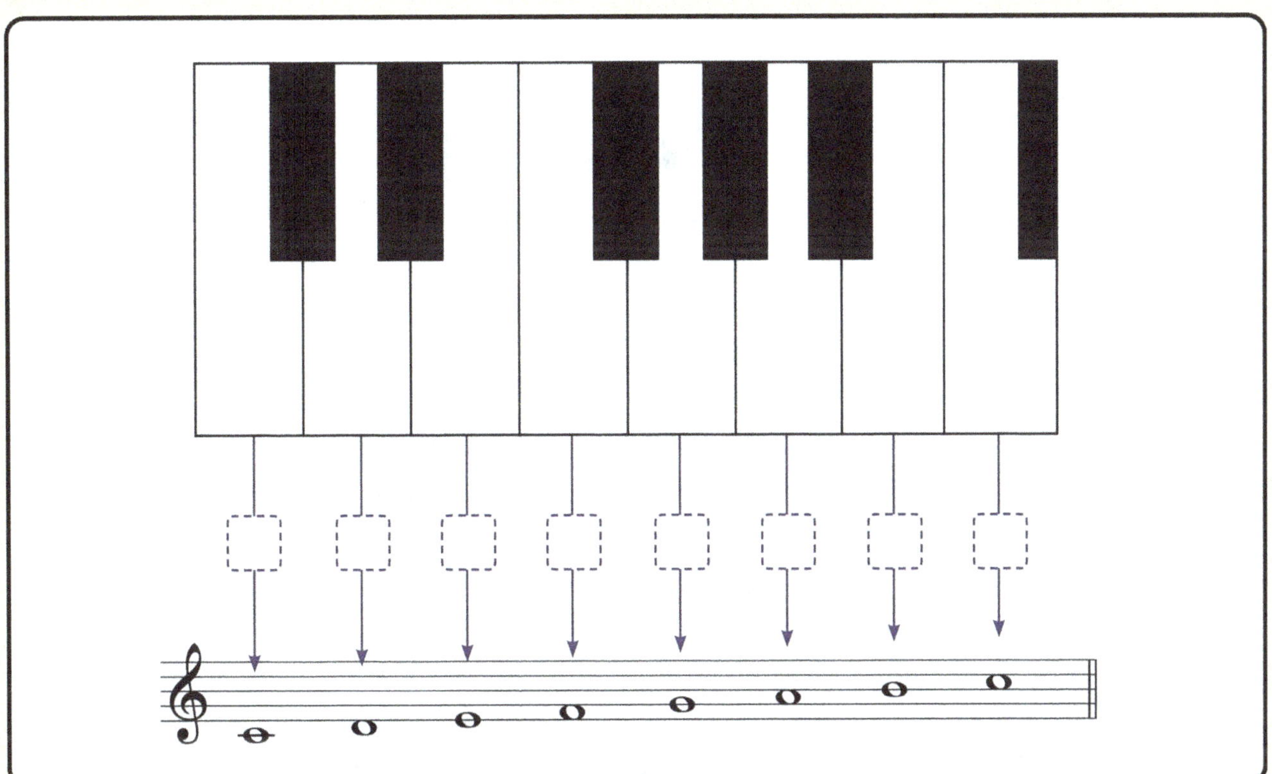

E Draw the treble clef and the C Major scale as you see it in the exercise above. Circle the notes on the lines in red and the ones in the spaces green.

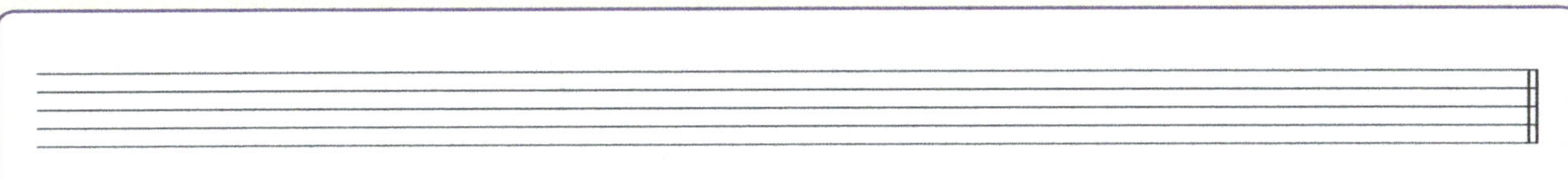

PRIMARY & ALTERED TONES

Tones are divided into primary and altered.

C, D, E, F, G, A, and B are the PRIMARY TONES. We play these tones on the white keys.
If we raise or lower any primary tone, we create an ALTERED TONE.

ALTERED TONES are created by changing the pitch of the primary tones. These altered tones can be either **raised** or **lowered**.

RAISED TONES

A raised tone has a higher pitch than its primary source. When we raise a primary tone by a half-step, we name it by adding the musical symbol to raise a tone # or its name - "**SHARP**" - after the altered primary tone's.

The names of the altered raised tones:
C# or sharp, D# or sharp, E# or sharp, F# or sharp, G# or sharp, A# or sharp, and B# or sharp.

To play an altered tone raised by a half-step on a keyboard,
we play the key closest to the primary tone we alter to the right, either black or white.

PRIMARY & ALTERED TONES

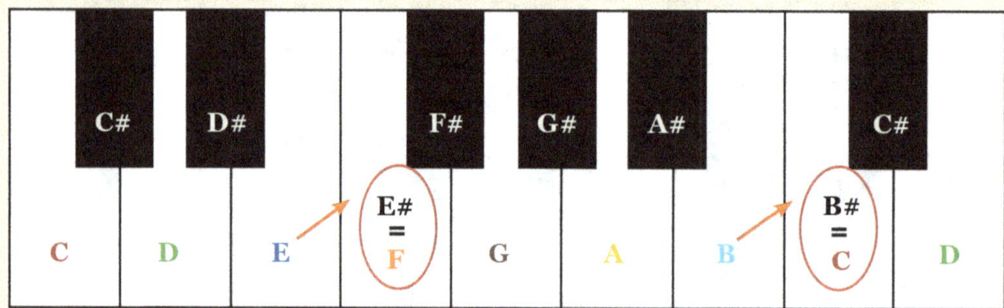

There are no black keys next to the notes **E** and **B**. The altered raised tones **E#** and **B#** don't have their black keys. When we raise **E** or **B** we must play the **white keys closest to them to the right**.
The tone **E#** is played on the primary tone **F** key and the **B#** on the primary tone **C** key.

E Write the name of the raised altered tones on the black keys.
Write the names of the keys we use to play tones E sharp and B sharp.

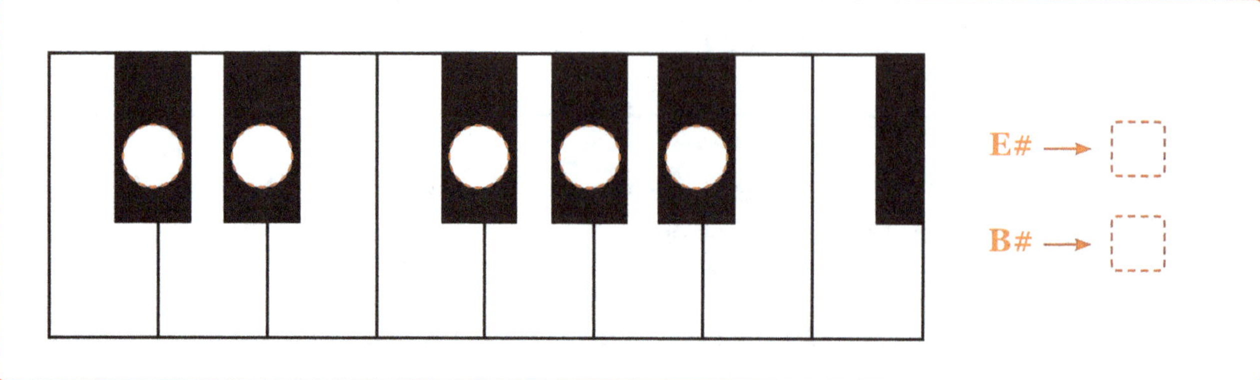

SHARPS AND NATURALS

Sharps and naturals are the musical symbols we call accidentals.

An accidental is a **musical symbol** that we place right before the note to raise or lower the **note's pitch** or cancel **previously imposed accidentals.**

The fundamental accidentals are:
SHARPS - the accidentals used to **raise the pitch** of a note by a **half-step.**
FLATS - the accidentals used to **lower the pitch** of a note by a **half-step.**
NATURALS - the accidentals that **cancel** previously imposed sharps or flats.

SHARP

A **sharp** is an accidental that **raises** the note's pitch by a **half-step.** If we wish to raise the pitch of a note by a half-step, we have to place the sharp right before it. The raised pitch is then applied to all notes of the same pitch within the measure.

NATURAL

A **natural** cancels the function of the sharp (or any other accidental).

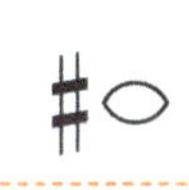

We must place the accidental **right in front** of the note we wish to alter. It has to be placed on the musical staff at exact place as the note we wish to alter. When **naming** the altered note, we use the name of the **note first** and **then** the **accidental** we used to alter it - C# or C sharp.

PRIMARY and ALTERED TONES (using sharps)

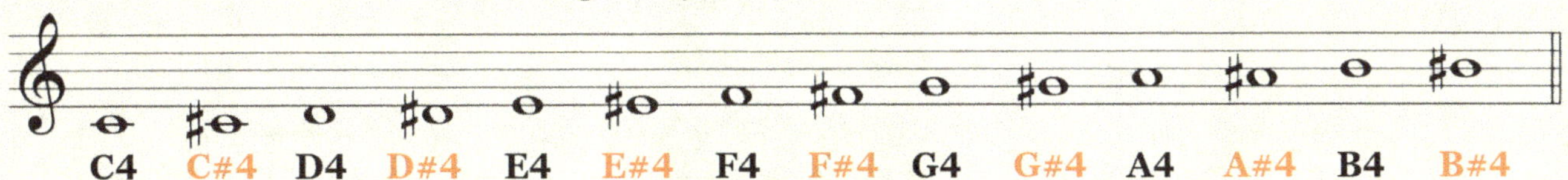

E Draw the accidentals according to the example. When drawing a sharp or a natural, we must ensure that the two short vertical lines define the height of the note we wish to alter.

REVIEW 1

NOTES and RESTS

E How long are the notes and rests?
Write the number of the beats in the squares below them.

NOTES ON THE MUSICAL STAFF

E Some notes are notated incorrectly. Circle them in red.

WHOLE STEP and HALF-STEP

E Connect frames that belong.

OCTAVES

E Mark the white keys with the name of the tone includings its octave number. The tone of the fifth octave circle in yellow

NOTES C4 - C6

E Draw the treble clef and the notes according to the names below the staff.

G4   B5   C5   A4   F5   E4   D5   C6   B4   A5

BASS CLEF

E Fill the cherries with the notes according to the names on their leaves.

TONES ALTERED UP USING SHARPS

While playing the C major scale raised half-step up - from **C#4** to **C#5** - we hear a row of tones similar to **C major**, only a **half-step higher**. It is the **C sharp major** scale.

E Write the name of the all half-step raised tone from *C#4* to *C#5*.

OCTAVES

E Write quarter notes based on the names, then write the names below the notes.

F#4   C#5   E#5   A#4   G#5   B#5   D#5   E#4   B#4   F#5

INTERVALS

An **INTERVAL** is the difference between the pitches of two tones or notes.
The primary intervals are derived from the distances between the first note and the other notes of a major scale. They are called unison, second, third, fourth, fifth, sixth, seventh, and octave.

The primary intervals are divided into PERFECT intervals and MAJOR intervals. Later, we will learn which intervals we call PERFECT and which MAJOR and how they differ.

Using the C major scale, let's learn the names of the primary intervals within the major scale.

PRIMARY INTERVALS OF THE C MAJOR SCALE

perfect unison - P1	two notes of the same pitch	C4 - C4
major second - M2	the distance between the first and the second tone	C4 - D4
major third - M3	the distance between the first and the third tone	C4 - E4
perfect fourth - P4	the distance between the first and the fourth tone	C4 - F4
perfect fifth - P5	the distance between the first and the fifth tone	C4 - G4
major sixth - M6	the distance between the first and the sixth tone	C4 - A4
major seventh - M7	the distance between the first and the seventh tone	C4 - B4
perfect octave - P8	the distance between the first and the eigth tone	C4 - C5

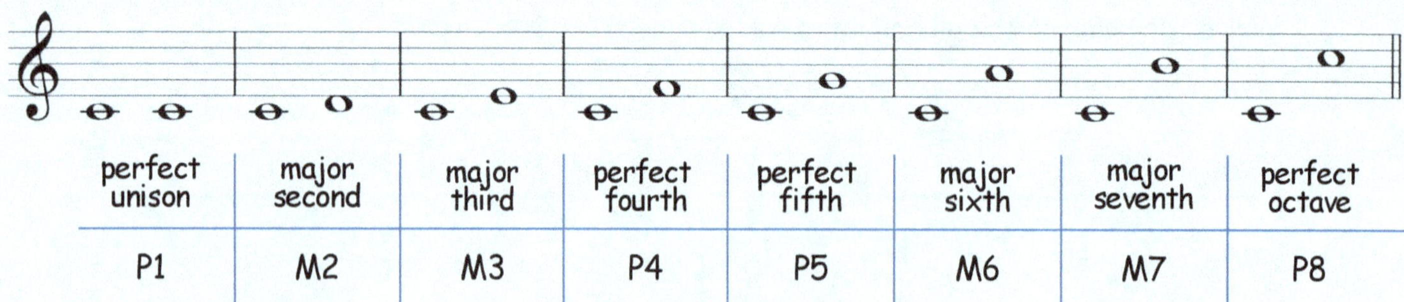

From this point forward, intervals will never leave us. We will use them to create scales, chords, melodies, and harmonies. Let's sing the **Interval Song** to help us learn to hear them.

INTERVAL SONG

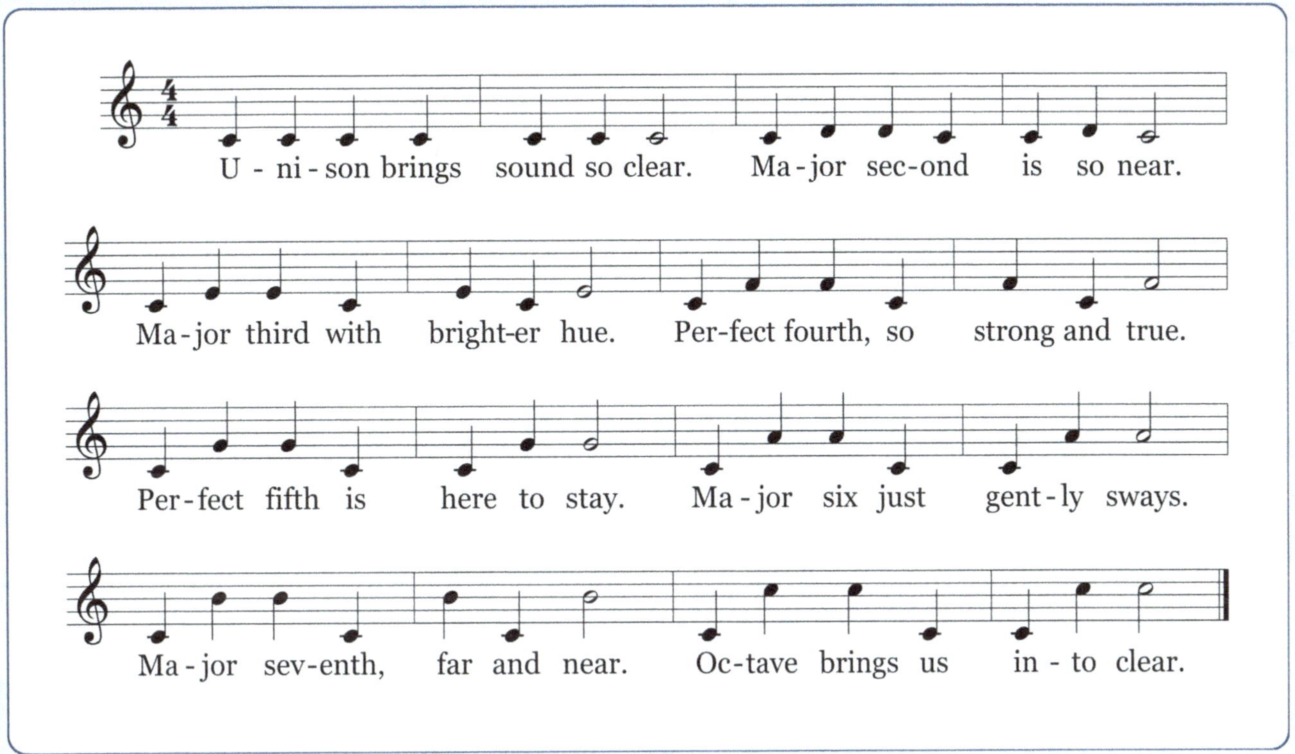

E Link belonging frames together. Assign a unique color to each interval.

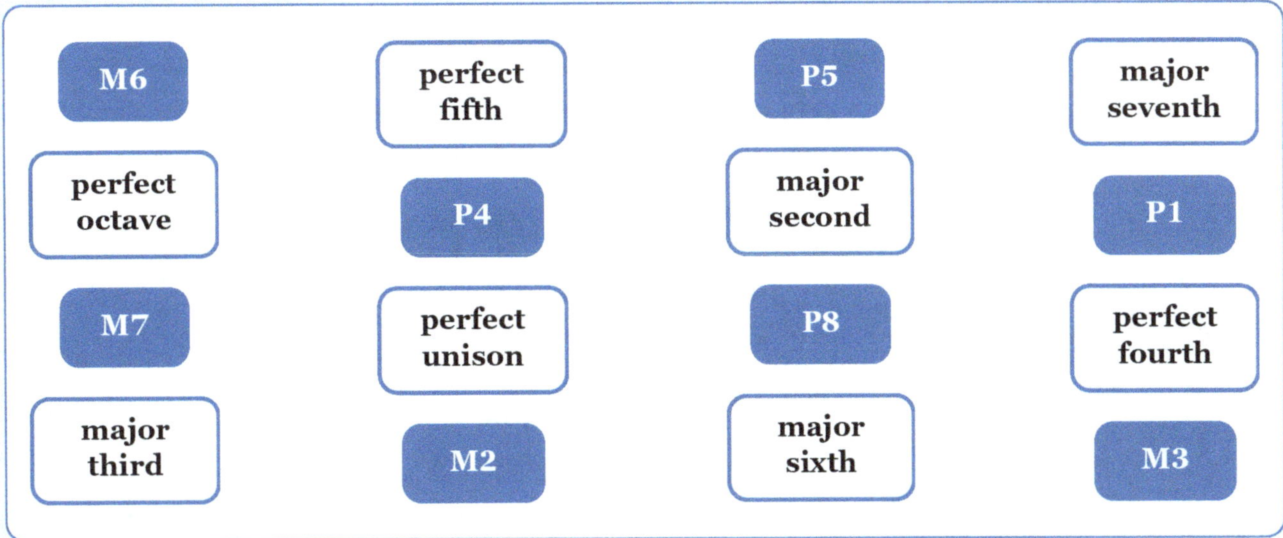

E Use the alphanumeric sign (P1, M3, etc.) to identify the interval in every measure.

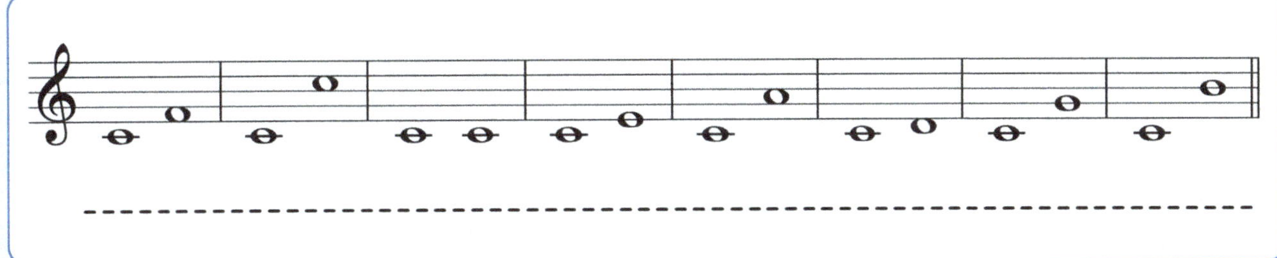

SCALES AND KEYS

A **SCALE** is a **row of tones** organized according to a preset structure.
The building blocks of the scale structure are whole steps and half-steps. To write down the structure of a scale, we use numbers: number 1 for whole steps and 1/2 for half-steps.

A **KEY** represents the **relationship of the tones within a piece with a particular scale**.
Keys have the same names as scales. For example, if we sing a song in the key of C major, we use tones from the C major scale - C, D, E, F, G, A, B, C - but not necessarily in that order, not always all of them, and some notes might be repeated several times.

There are many different scales and keys, with the primary ones being major and minor.
Typically, simple children's folk songs are composed in major keys.

MAJOR SCALE

We already know that the primary major scale is C major.
The structure of a major scale consists of five whole steps and two half-steps. The half-steps are between the third and fourth and the seventh and eighth tones of the scale.

The major scale's structure shown using numbers for whole steps and half-steps.

| 1 | 1 | 1/2 | 1 | 1 | 1 | 1/2 |

The same structure applies to all **major scales regardless of their keys**. As you can see, a major scale is built from two identical building blocks each made of **two whole steps** and **one half-step** separated by a **whole step**. We call these blocks **TETRACHORDS**.

TETRA - four
CHORD - a cluster of tones

C MAJOR SCALE STRUCTURE
STEPS AND TETRACHORDS

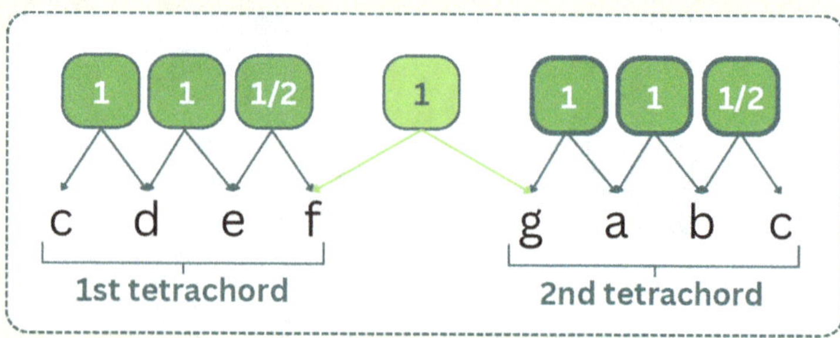

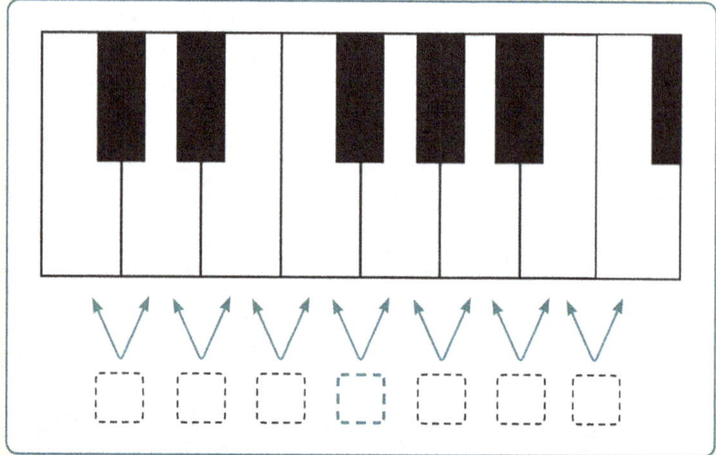

E Write numbers indicating whole steps and half steps into the squares below the two keys. You should get the structure of two identical tetrachords of a major scale.

CHORDS

CHORD

A **chord** is a combination of three or more tones.
The most common chord is **a TRIAD**, which is a chord made of **three tones**.

FIFTH CHORD

The **fifth chord** is the most commonly used chord. It consists of the root tone, its third, and fifth. Its name is derived from the interval between the bottom and top notes - the perfect fifth.

TONIC FIFTH CHORD

The **tonic fifth chord** is the primary chord of any major scale. It's built on the root tone, followed by the third note (the major third) and the fifth tone (the perfect fifth).
We call it **TONIC** because the root tone has a harmonic function defining the tonality, the home base of the scale - the TONIC. We mark it with the letter **T**.

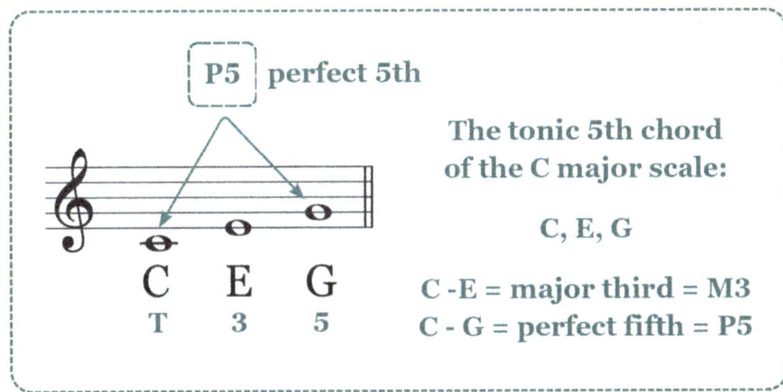

MELODIC AND HARMONIC FIFTH CHORD

The **MELODIC FIFTH CHORD** sounds like a melody.
It's tones are played or sung consecutively in ascending or descending motion.

ascending melodic tonic fifth chord

descending melodic tonic fifth chord

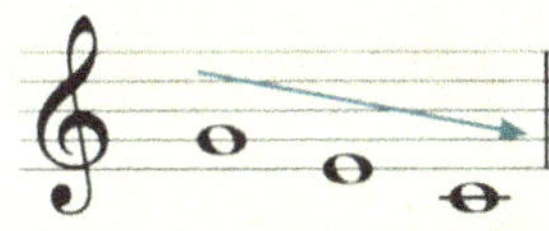

The **HARMONIC FIFTH CHORD** is played or sung with all its notes at the same time. It's commonly used for simple accompaniment of songs.

E Write the names of the notes, find the C tonic fifth chord, then circle it read.

MAJOR SCALES WITH SHARPS

A major scale can start from any tone, not just from C. The only thing that remains unchanged is the **major scale whole steps and half-steps structure**. Therefore, because all the primary tones were used while creating the C major scale, some notes have to be altered - **raised or lowered**.

The major scales with raised tones - altered using sharps - **are the major scales with sharps.**

MAJOR SCALES WITH SHARPS

G major, D major, A major, E, major, B major, F# major, **and** C# major.

- The first major scale with sharps starts on **the fifth step of the C major scale**.
- The C major scale is the primary major scale without accidentals.
- Every next scale starts on **the fifth step** of the previous scale.
- Every next scale has one more sharp added to **its seventh step**.
- The sharps are added in this order: **F#, C#, G#, D#, A#, E#,** and **B#**.

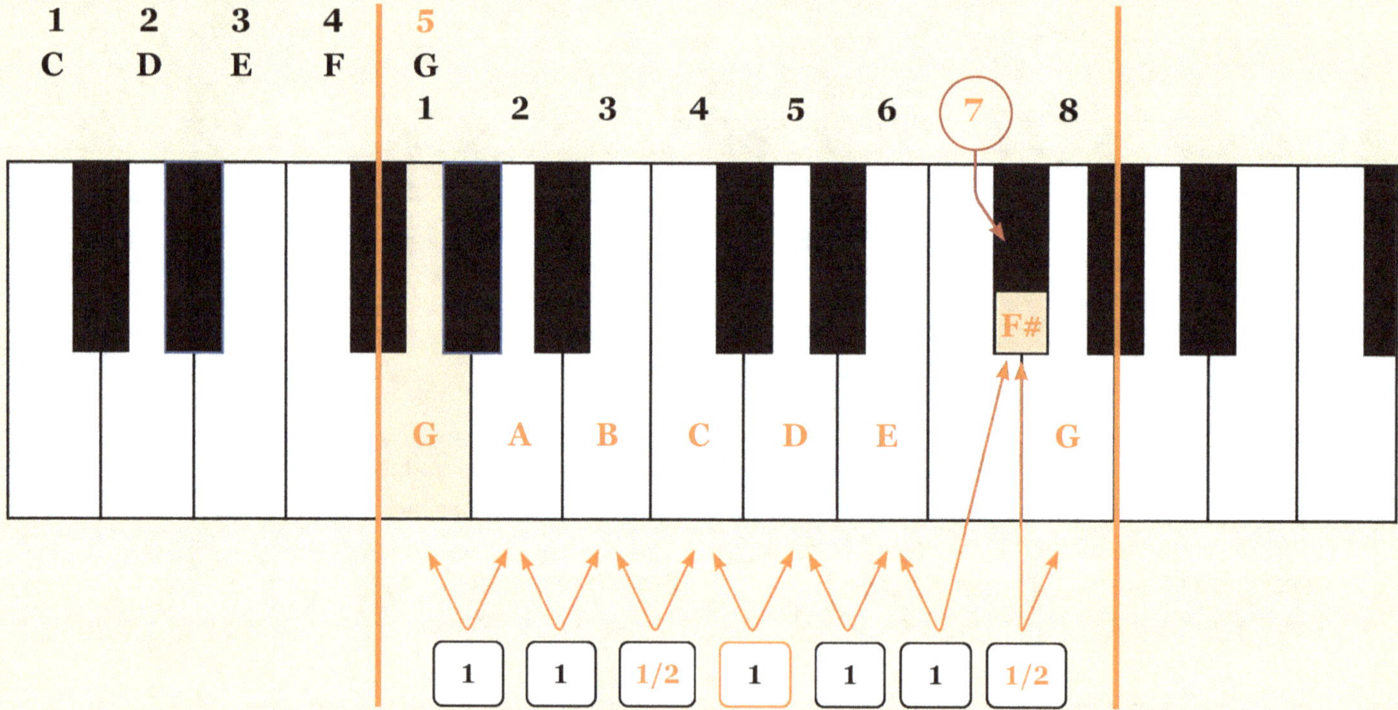

Let's test what we learned by building the first major scale with sharps.
(Use the staff paper at thee end of the book.)

- *We start with the primary major scale, the C major scale (no accidentals).*
- *We learned that the next scale starts on C major's **fifth step - tone G**.*
- *G is the root tone of the next scale. We should end up building **the G major scale**.*
- *We start by writing down the row of tones we know from C major but starting from G up:*
  G, A, B, C, D, E, F, G.
- *To preserve the structure of a major scale - **1-1-1/2-1-1-1-1/2** - we must **raise the new scale's seventh step** using a **sharp** - F to F#.*
- *The tones of the new scale are **G, A, B, C, D, E,** F# - G major, with one sharp, F#.*

KEY SIGNATURE

The **KEY SIGNATURE** is a set of accidentals that tells us the key of the piece by a **designated number of accidentals** - sharps OR flats.

The key signature is always placed **right after the clef on every single staff.**

The accidentals within the key signature are marked in **a strictly designated order.**

MAJOR SCALES WITH SHARPS KEY SIGNATURES

Every scale has a different number of sharps - **a different key signature.**

The sharps must be marked in designated order: **F#, C#, G#, D#, A#, E#,** and **B#.**

F, C, G, D, A, E, B
In the row in their right places
Sharps are flocking behind the clef
Like their notes on lines and spaces

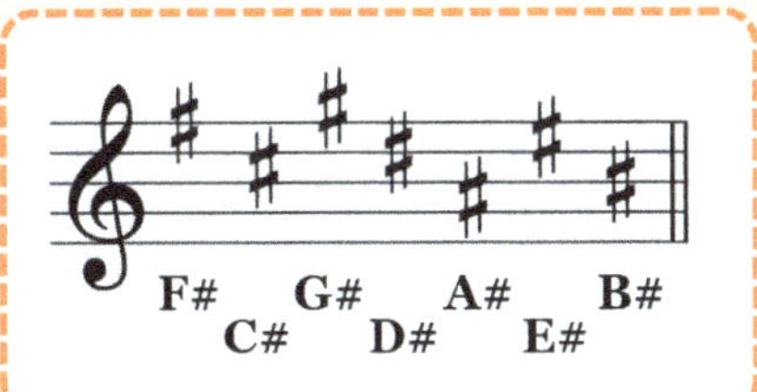

SUMMARY

*The set of sharps at the beginning of a piece is called **the key signature.***
*The key signature tells us **the tonality** of the piece.*
*The key signature must be present at the beginning of **every staff of the piece**
right after the clef.*
*The accidentals within the key signature apply to **all equally named notes** of the piece.*

E   Copy the sharps in the correct order, then write their names on the line below.

MAJOR SCALES WITH SHARPS

The first major scale with sharps is the C major scale (it has no sharps).
The following major scales with sharps start on the fifth step of the previous scale.
Every new scale has one more sharp than the scale before it.
The sharps are added in the strictly given order as follows: F#, C#, G#, D#, A#, E#, and B#.

To better visualized the progression of the scale we use
the diagram called the CIRCLE OF FIFTHS.

Learn and memorize the MAJOR SCALES WITH SHARPS
C major, G major, D major, A major,
E major, B major, F# major, C# major.

> **Poem of Major Scales with Sharps**
> Cats know purring, meowing, stretching
> Geese feast on the grass
> Dogs are really good at fetching
> Elephants are a giant class
> Antelopes are on the move
> Bisons standing still
> F and C are the last two sharped scales
> Now, go practice your new skill!

To better visualized the progression of the scale we use
the diagram called the CIRCLE OF FIFTHS.

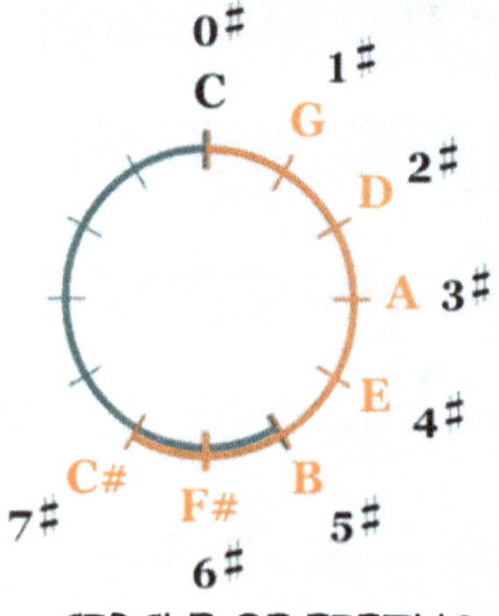

CIRCLE OF FIFTHS

1♯
G
2♯
D
3♯
A
4♯
E
5♯
B

CONSTRUCTING MAJOR SCALES WITH SHARPS

MAJOR SCALES WITH SHARPS

- The first major scale with sharps is the **C major** scale.
- The following major scales with sharps start on the **fifth step** of the previous scale.
- Every new scale has **one more sharp** than the scale before it.
- The new sharp is applied to **the seventh step** of the new scale.

MAJOR SCALES WITH SHARPS UP TO 4SHARPS

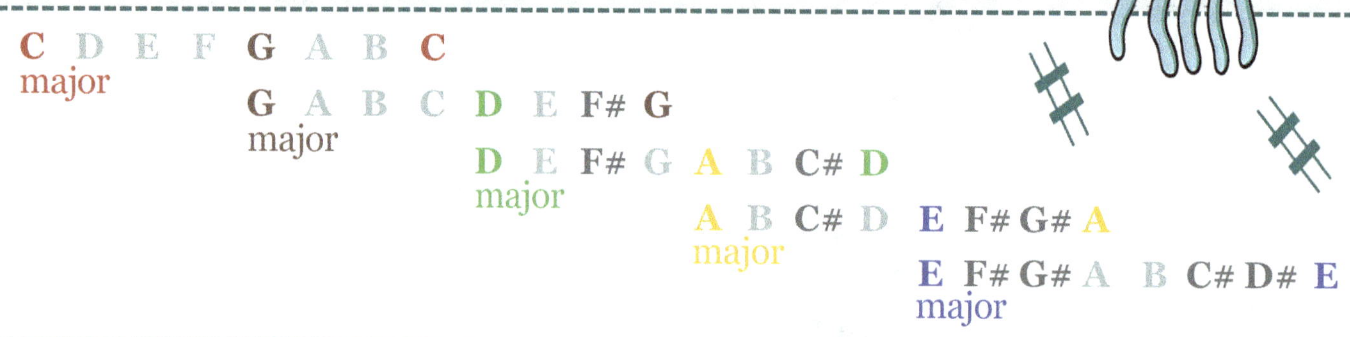

- **The circle of fifths** shows us the progression of the major scales with sharps. The name of the diagram tells us that each scale starts on **the fifth** step of the previous scale.
- The sharps are added in the following order:
  F#, C#, G#, D#, A#, E#, B#.
- The first C major scale **has now key signature**
  The last C# major scale **has seven sharps.**
- **Tetrachords:** a major scale can be divided into two equal parts we call **tetrachords.** Both tetrachords are built from **two whole steps and one half-step,** in that exact order, and are **separated by a whole step.**

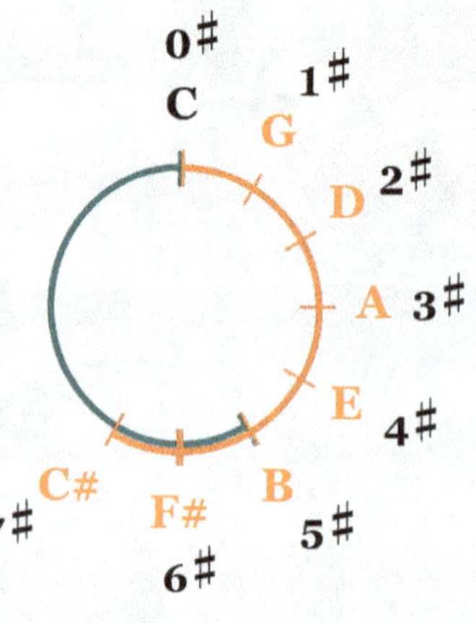

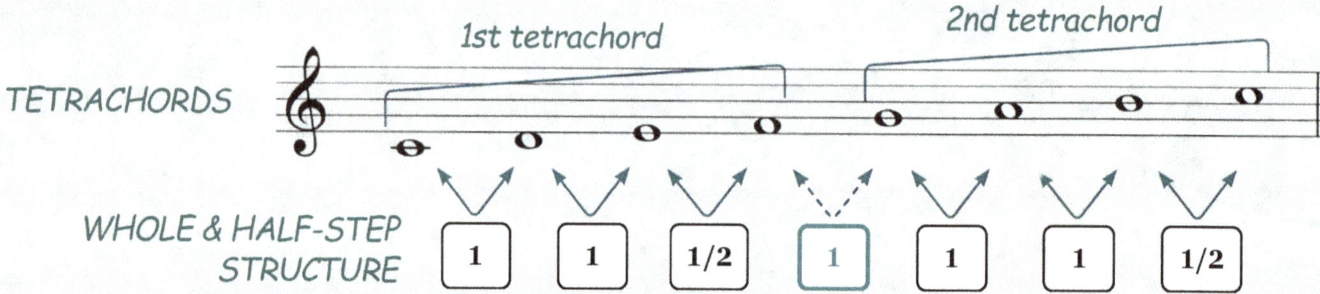

| E | List the names of all major scales with sharps, following the Circle of Fifths. Then, draw all the sharps in the correct sequence as they appear in the key signature. |

G MAJOR SCALE

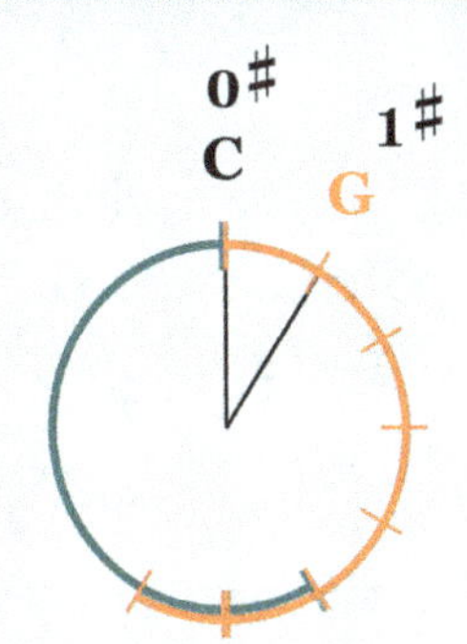

- The **G major scale** starts on the note **G**.
- The note **G** is the fifth note of the previous C major scale.
- The major scales with sharps: C, **G**, D, A, E, B, F#, C#

Memorize the notes of the G major scale in the ascending and descending motion:

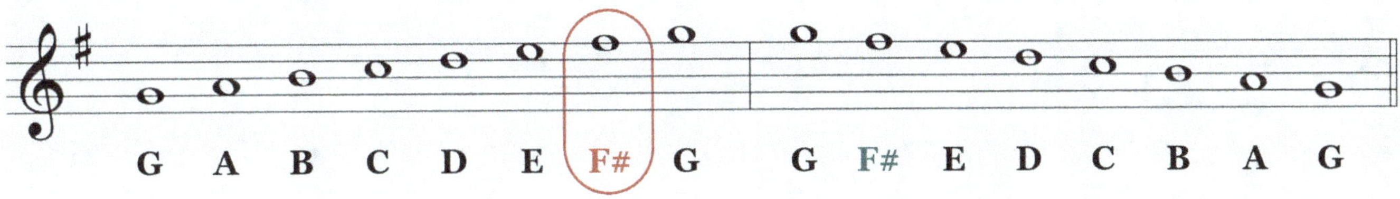

- **The G major tonic fifth chord is G, B, D. Its chord designation is G.**

melodic G major fifth chord   *harmonic G major fifth chord*

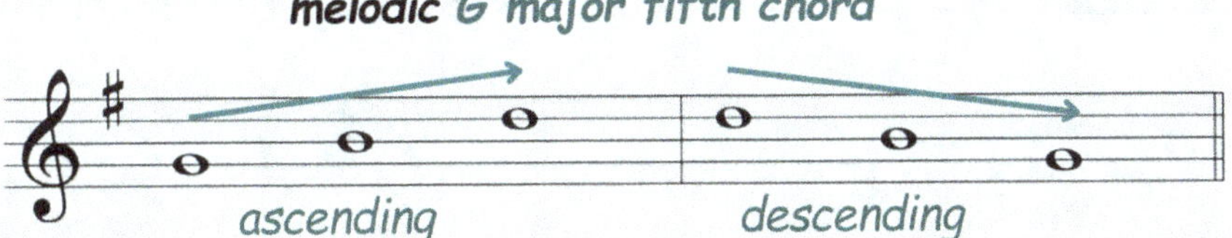

E | Write the names of the notes on the lines below them. Notice the red brackets indicating the half-steps and the blue ones indicating the triads.

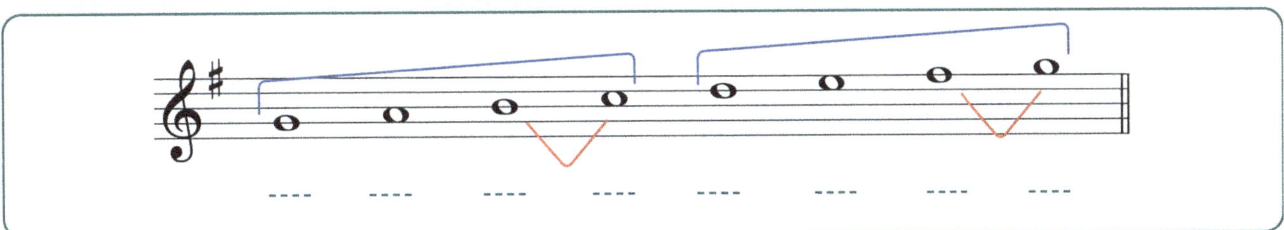

E | Notice the key signature in the song "I'm From a Village High Above." Write the name of the sharp and the chord symbol on the lines, then circle all the notes altered by the accidental.

Sharp(s): ___________________________   *Key:* _________

Clefi & Notelina's Songbook, pg. 47

D MAJOR SCALE

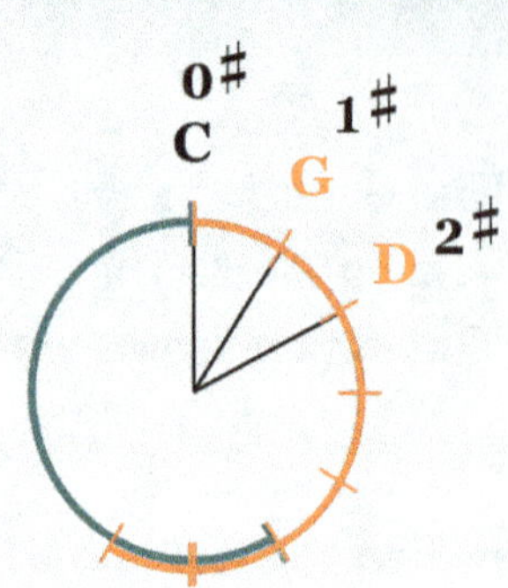

- The **D major** scale starts on the note D.
- The note **D** is the fifth note of the previous G major scale.
- The major scales with sharps: C, G, **D**, A, E, B, F#, C#

Memorize the notes of the D major scale in the
ascending and descending motion:

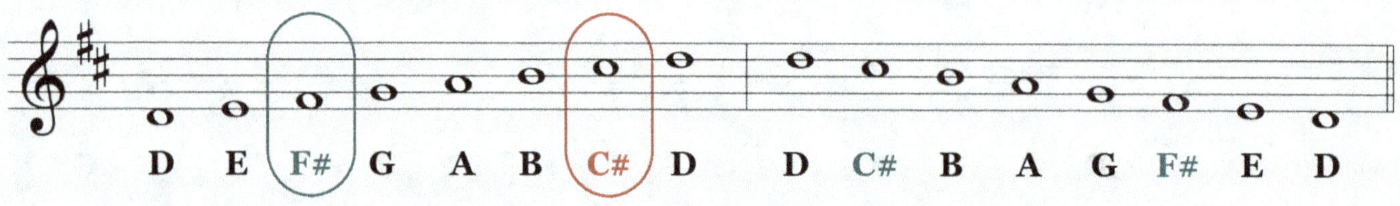

- **The D major tonic fifth chord is D, F#, A. Its chord designation is D.**

melodic *D major fifth chord*   **harmonic** *D major fifth chord*

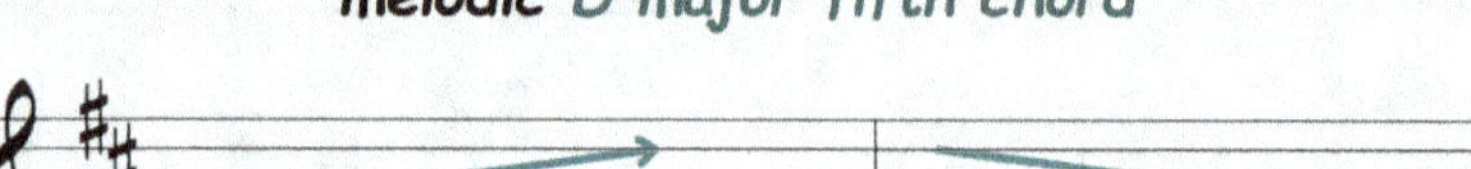

E Write the D major scale using the key signature. Use red brackets to identify the half-steps and blue brackets to mark the tetrachords, as you saw on the previous page.

E Notice the key signature in the song "Used to Be Well Then." Write the name of the sharps and the chord symbol on the lines, then circle all the notes altered by the accidental.

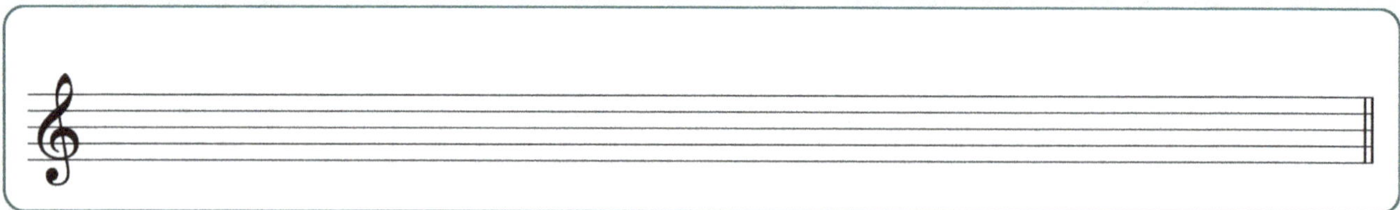

A MAJOR SCALE

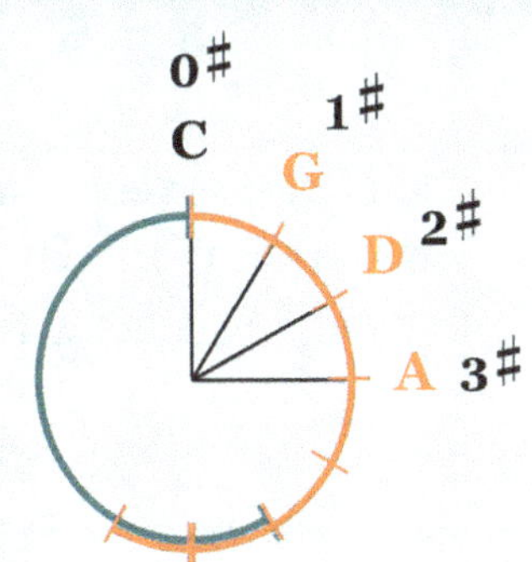

- The **A major** scale starts on the note **A**.
- The note **A** is the fifth note of the previous D major scale.
- The major scales with sharps: C, G, D, **A**, E, B, F#, C#

Memorize the notes of the A major scale in the ascending and descending motion:

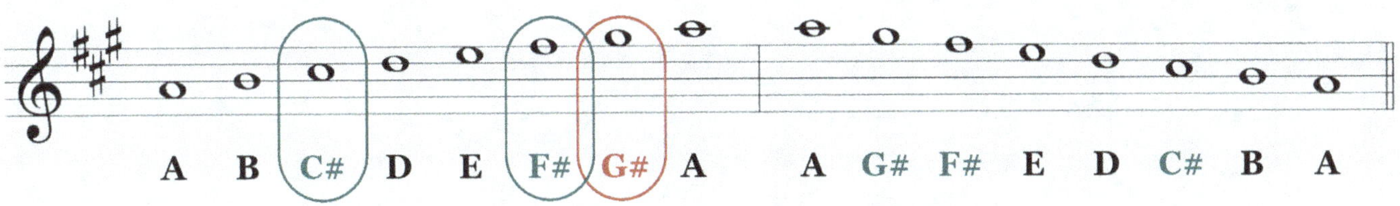

- **The A major tonic fifth chord is A, C#, E. It's chord designation is A.**

melodic A major fifth chord

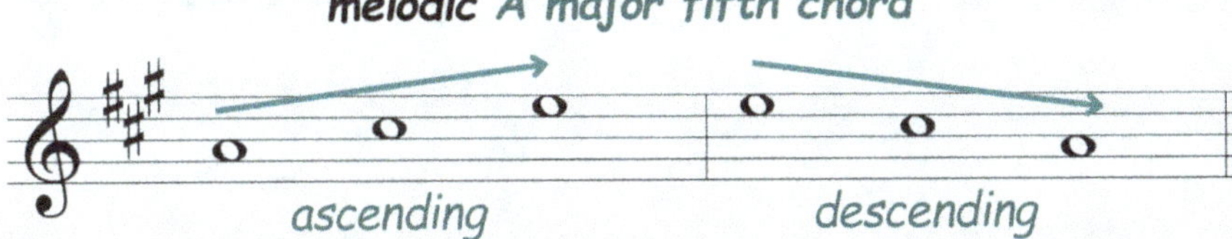

harmonic A major fifth chord

E Write the A major scale using the key signature. Use red brackets to identify the half-steps and blue brackets to mark the tetrachords, as you saw on the previous pages.

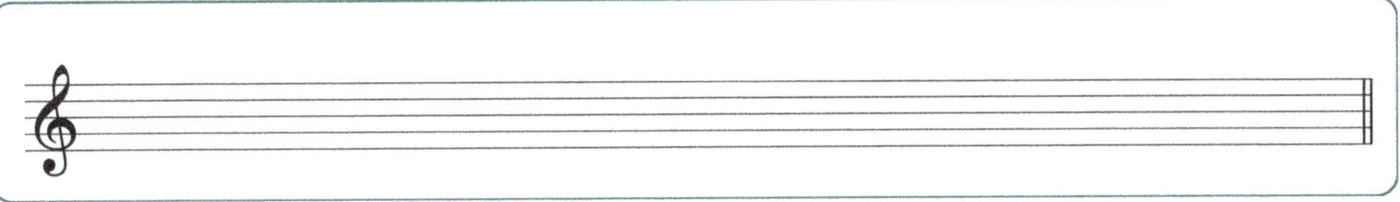

E Notice the key signature in the song "When I Passed the City Gate." Write the name of the sharps and the chord symbol on the lines, then mark notes a half-step apart with red brackets.

Clefi & Notelina's Songbook, pg. 50

Sharp(s): _______________________________ *Key:* _________

E MAJOR SCALE

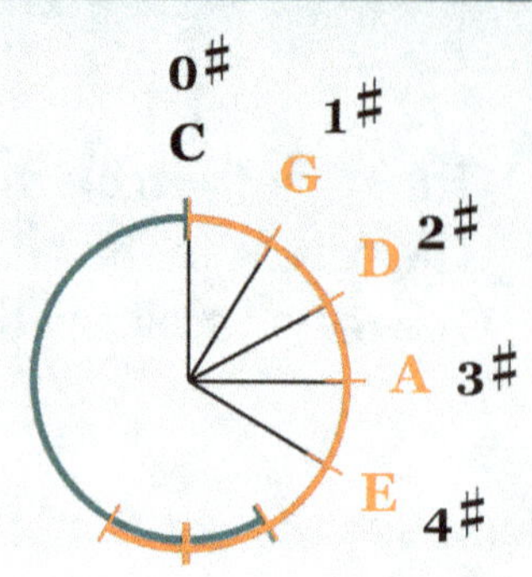

- The E major scale starts on the note E.
- The note E is the fifth note of the previous A major scale.
- The major scales with sharps: C, G, D, A, E, B, F#, C#

Memorize the notes of the E major scale in the ascending and descending motion:

- **The E major tonic fifth chord is E, G#, B. Its chord designation is E.**

melodic E major fifth chord

harmonic E major fifth chord

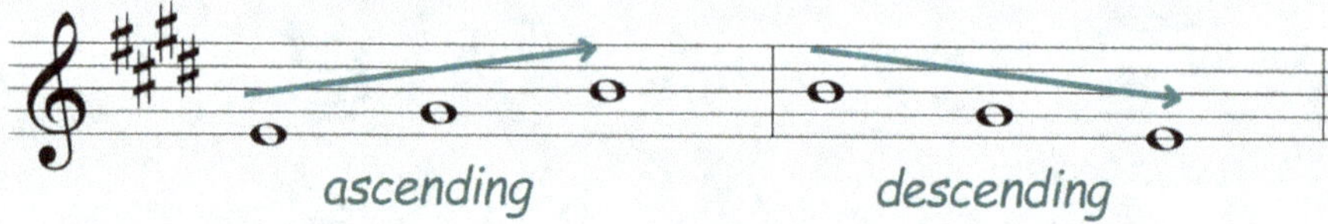

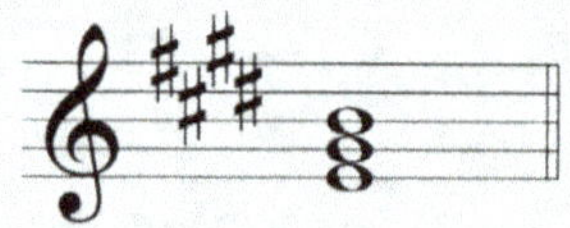

E Write the E major scale using the key signature. Use red brackets to identify the half-steps and blue brackets to mark the tetrachords.

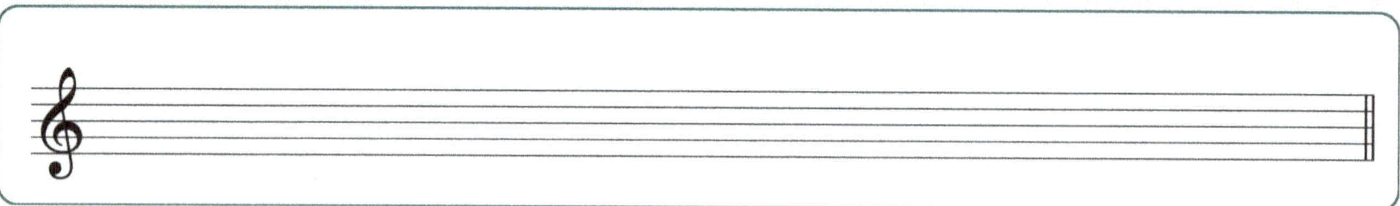

E Connect the pots that belong, color them with the same color.

REVIEW 2

E Be a detective and find the correct key signature for each example. Start by writing down the name of the key derived from the root note of the tonic fifth chord.

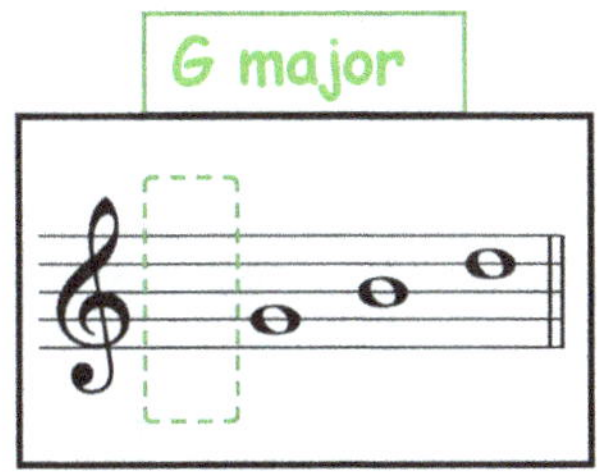

TRANSPOSITION

Transposition is moving a song or a piece from one key to another.
When we write, sing, or play a song or a piece in a different key than originally composed, we call it **transposing**.

E Transpose the opening phrase of the song "Little Turtle Dove" from C major to the two keys that you must first correctly identify.

1. Get familiar with the opening of the song in its original key.
2. Identify the key by reading the key signature and the root note, then write it down.
3. Follow the structure of the notes by assigning the notes to numbers in the new key with the root note of the new key being new 1. (C major = 1 is C, G major = 1 is G,...)
4. Write down the notes for both transposed opening phrases of the song "Little Turtle Dove" and check your results by playing them in the new key.

Clefi & Notelina's Songbook, pg. 18

Key: C major

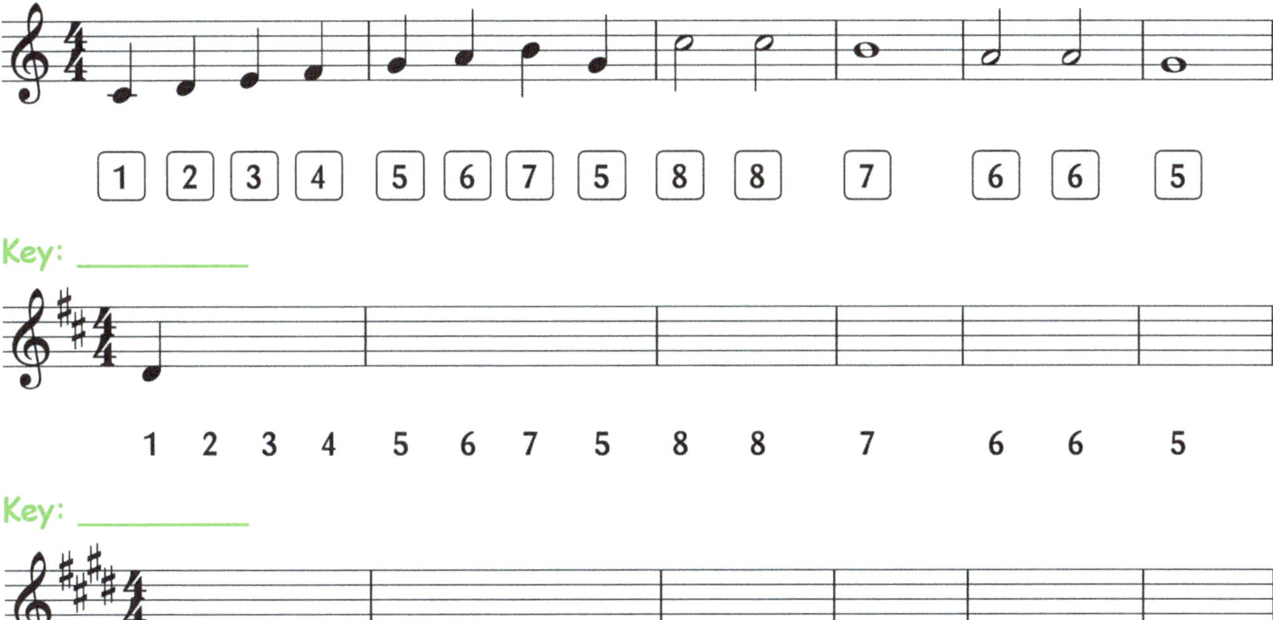

| 1 | 2 | 3 | 4 | 5 | 6 | 7 | 5 | 8 | 8 | 7 | 6 | 6 | 5 |

Key: _________

1 2 3 4 5 6 7 5 8 8 7 6 6 5

Key: _________

TONE VOLUME - DYNAMICS

We can play tones at **various volumes: loudly, softly, or somewhere in between**. The loudness of tones and the symbols that indicate how loudly we should play are referred to as DYNAMICS.

DYNAMIC SYMBOLS

Dynamic symbols indicate the **volume** needed to perform a piece or song. Each dynamic symbol remains in effect until a new one appears, which either reinforces or alters the dynamics. The names and markings of these dynamic symbols have their roots in Italian, which is why we refer to it as **Italian musical terminology.**

To simplify the marking and reading process, we utilize abbreviated notations that represent the full Italian musical terms, such as *p, pp, ppp, f, mf,* and so on.

tone volume	symbol	Italian term	pronunciation
very softly	*pp*	pianissimo	pee-uh-**ni**-suh-mow
softly	*p*	**piano**	pee-**a**-now
medium softly	*mp*	mezzopiano	**meh**-tso pee-**a**-now
medium strong	*mf*	mezzoforte	**meh**-tso **for**-tay
strong	*f*	**forte**	**for**-tay
very strong	*ff*	fortissimo	for-**ti**-suh-mow

The tone volume can also increase and decrease **gradually**.

Crescendo (kruh-**shen**-dow) means to get gradually stronger (louder). We can abbreviate it as "**cresc.**"
Decrescendo (dee-kruh-**shen**-dow) means to get gradually softer. It is abbreviated as "**decresc.**"

Crescendo and decrescendo can also be marked using "hairpins."
The opening hairpin marks crescendo, and the closing hairpin marks decrescendo.

crescendo   *decrescendo*

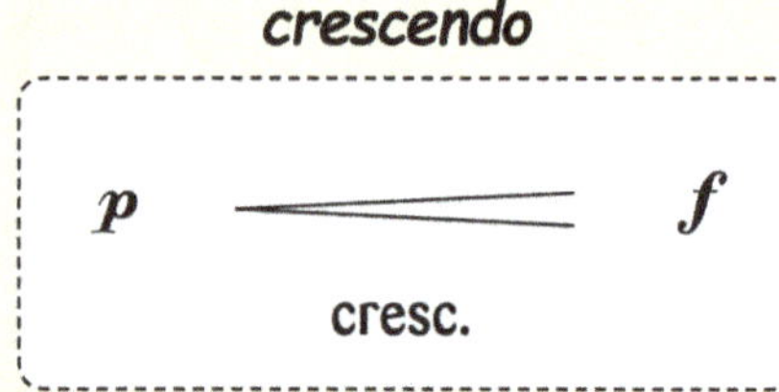

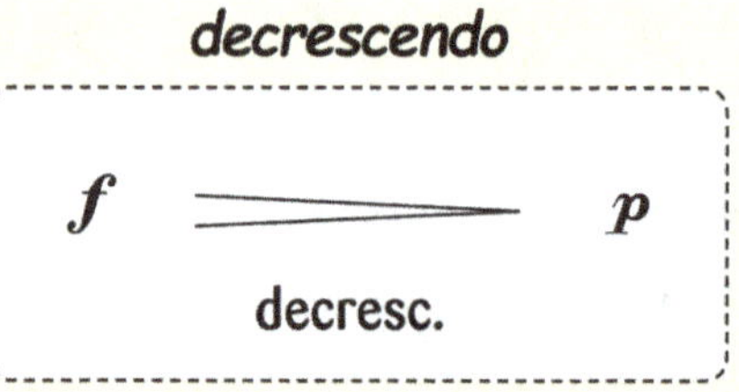

TONE CHARACTER - ARTICULATION

Even though a tone is determined by the note's value, its ultimate sound relies on the character - ARTICULATION - assigned by the composer or arranger. We perform the tones either **shorter or at full value, connected or separated**, based on this specified character. The symbols and markings that define tone character are referred to as ARTICULATION **markings and symbols**.

Most common **articulation** markings are *staccato*, *tenuto*, and *legato*.

character: **staccato** (stuh-**kaa**-tow) = **pointy short**
execution: tones are **separated** and **very short**
symbol or marking: a **dot** above or blow the note or by the abbreviation **"stacc."**

character: **tenuto** (tuh-**noo**-tow) = held for the **full note value**
execution: tones are played **without decay** and with minimal **separation**
symbol or marking: most often not marked or reinforced by a short line above or below the note or by the abbreviation **"ten."**

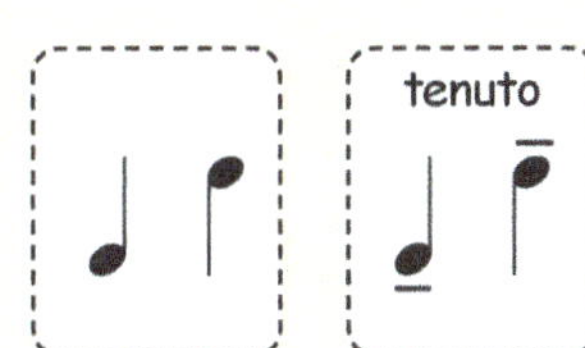

character: **legato** (luh-**gaa**-tow) = **connected**
execution: two or more tones are connected in one breath, bow, or gesture
symbol or marking: **a slur** (a curved line) connecting all the notes meant to be sung or played without separation or re-articulation

E Examine the opening phrases of "A Little Vixen Under a Tree" and "Little Cuckoo Bird." Describe the character of the articulations used in both sections and name them above the notation.

Clefi & Notelina's Songbook, pg. 26   *Clefi & Notelina's Songbook, pg. 54*

E Examine closely the song "Little Cuckoo bird." Find all articulations and dynamics and name them. Circle the soft dynamics in red and the loud ones in yellow. Then try to play or sing the song observing all the markings. *Clefi & Notelina's Songbook, pg. 54*

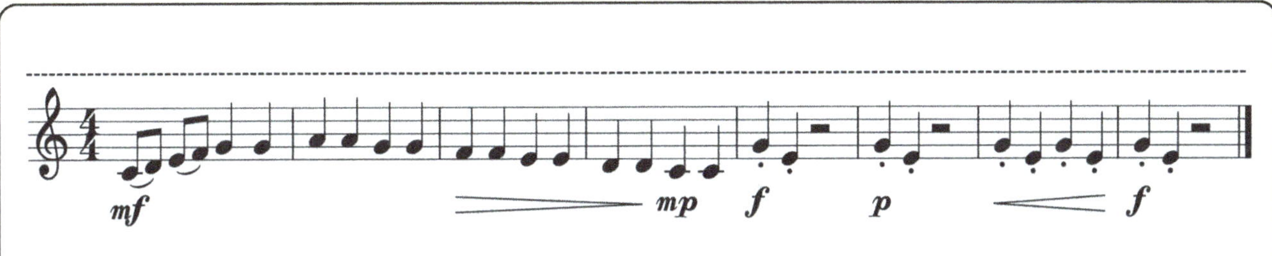

NOTATION MARKINGS

REPEAT SIGN

The repeat sign is a musical symbol that indicates a specific section or piece should be repeated. Its placement informs musicians where to return and which measure to start the repetition. If there is no repeat sign marking the beginning of the repeated section, we begin again from the begining of the piece or song.

The repeat sign consists of **two vertical lines of different thickness positioned across the staff, and two dots located in the third and fourth spaces**. The symbol's placement indicates both the start and end points of the repeated section.

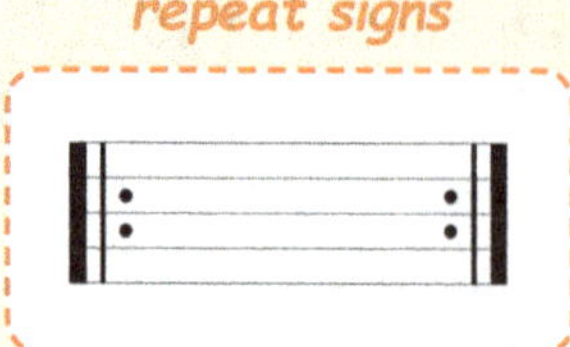

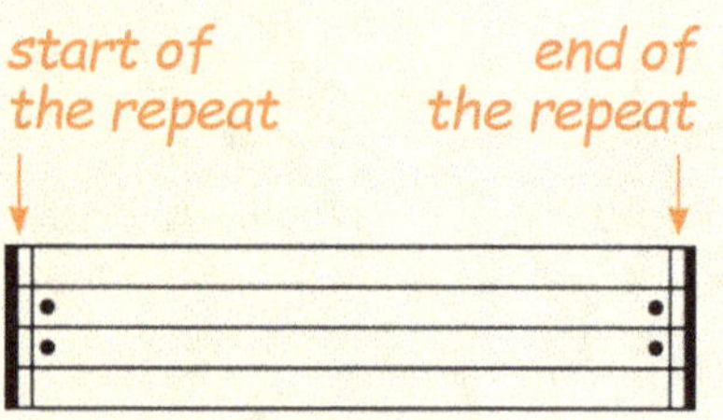

E Copy the repeat signs.

FERMATA

The fermata symbol signifies the desired **prolongation of a note or rest**. Generally, the fermata prolongs the note or rest that carries the symbol by at least half its original value; however, there are no strict guidelines dictating exactly how long the note should be held.

TIE

A tie is a curved line that **links two notes of the same pitch**. Its purpose is **to extend the duration** of the first note by the value of the second tied note. This means the first note is played **seamlessly, without any interruption**.

E Analyze the song "If There Only Were Some." Tell the difference between a legato and a tie. Circle the notes with ties in green and those with legato in blue. Write the number of measures in the song as notated and how many when sung with all the repeats.

Clefi & Notelina's Songbook, pg. 52

RHYTHM AND METER

RHYTHM

Rhythm is an important element of music. It has always been linked to walking and dancing.

HEAVY BEATS

As we clap and sing together, we naturally identify certain beats that stand out as more important. You may notice that we **emphasize** these beats by making them **more prominent**, possibly by stomping or clapping louder. We call these highlighted moments **ACCENTED** or **HEAVY BEATS**.

Accented beats can occur anywhere in a song.
Accents are small empty arrowheads above or below the note.

The heavy beats are closely tied to the rhythm of a piece or song, consistently marking **the initial beats** of each measure. The fundamental rhythmic division is **two** or **three beats per measure**.

two-beat rhythm (two syllables)

ta-ble / *doc*-tor / *kit*-ten

three-beat rhythm (three syllables)

in-ter-net / *ba*-na-na / *a*-nim-al

E Find words representing two and three-beat rhythmical patterns. (i.e. tab-le / ba-na-na)

MEASURE

Measures are small sections of the musical notation of a piece or a song separated by **measure lines (bar lines)**. The first beat of the measure is typically the heavy - **the downbeat**. The fundamental unit of the measure is **a beat**. A beat can be represented by a note of any value - a quarter note, an eighth note, a half note, and so on.

TIME SIGNATURE - METER

The time signature, or meter, consists of two stacked numbers and is located at the beginning of a piece, **immediately following the clef**. It indicates how to count the individual measures in the musical notation.

- upper number = number of beats in the measure
- lower number = the note value of the beat (4 = the quarter note, 8 = the eighth note, and so on.)

Time signatures 4/4/ and 2/2 can also use designation 𝄴 = 4/4 and 𝄵 = 2/2.

E Write the number of the beats in the upper squares and draw the correct note in the lower squares.

3	3	*number of beats*	3		2		4		6	
4	♩	*note value*	8		4		4		8	

SIMPLE & COMBINED MEASURES

Measures are SIMPLE and COMBINED.

SIMPLE MEASURE

Simple measures have only one **heavy beat - the downbeat**.
The remaining beats are considered the **light beats**.
All two-beat and three-beat measures (2/4, 2/8, 3/4, 3/8, etc.) are SIMPLE MEASURES.

Counting Beats in Simple Measures

In simple measure, we count all the beats indicated by the upper number of the time signature.
The basic unit is a beat regardless of the note value, which is indicate by the lower number.
We count the beats like this: one, two, (three) or one-and, two-and, (three-and).

Two-four Measure 2/4
The beat is **a quarter note**.
The measure has two beats

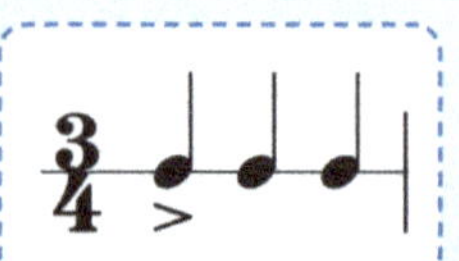

Three-four Measure 3/4
The beat is **a quarter note**.
The measure has three beats.

E Fill in the time signature according to the number of beats in measures. Mark the heavy beats.

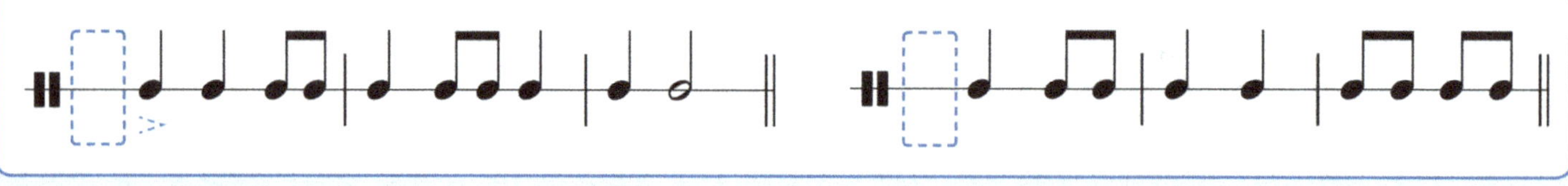

Three-eighth Measure 3/8
The beat is **a eighth note**.
The measure has three beats.

E Learn to sing or play the new song about a swallow in the 3/8 measure. Mark all the heavy beats.

COMBINED MEASURES

Combined measures are measures with **more than three beats**. We can build them by combining **several simple measures**. The combined measure has the heavy beat on the first beat - **the downbeat** - and one or more **secondary heavy beats**. The most common examples of the combined measure in music are the four-four (4/4) and six-eighth (6/8) measures.

When indicating the downbeat in the combined measure, we use the musical symbol for "accent." 

When indicating the secondary heavy beat in the combined measure, we use the musical symbol for "tenuto." 

Example: **4/4 rhythm** *can be divided into two 2/4 ones.*
The main beat is on **the downbeat**, *the secondary heavy beat on* **the 3rd. beat.**

door is clos-ing / car is mov-ing / dog is bark-ing / cat is meow-ing

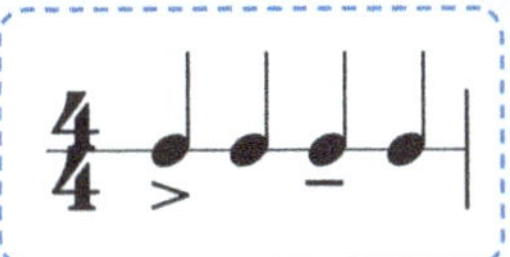

Four-four Measure 4/4

The four-four time or meter is also called **common time**. It can also be marked by a symbol "**C.**"
The beat in the 4/4 measure is **a quarter note**.
The measure has **four beats**.
The 4/4 measure is a combined measure built from **two 2/4 measures**. Besides the downbeat, its has the secondary heavy beat on **the third beat**.

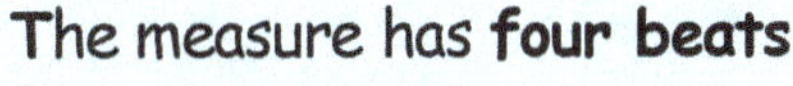

E Mark all the downbeats and secondary heavy beats.

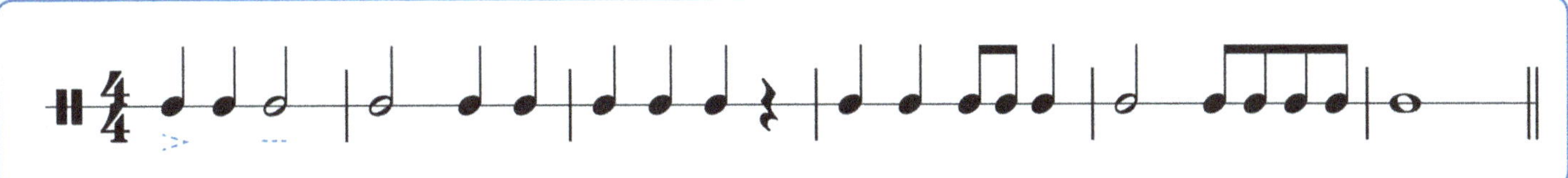

Six-eighth Measure 6/8

The beat in the 6/8 measure is **an eighth note**.
The measure has **six beats**.
The 6/8 measure is a combined measure built from **two 3/8 measures**. Besides the downbeat, it has the secondary heavy beat on **the fourth beat**.

E Learn to sing or play the new song about a bagpiper in the 6/8 measure. Mark **all** heavy beats.

DOTS AFTER NOTES

A dot after a note **increases the note's value by half**.
The same applies to rests.
The dot changes the name of a note or rest to **"dotted."**

The **dot** is always placed **after** a **note** or a **rest**.
If we place a dot after a note or a rest, **their value changes**.
It increases by **half of the initial value** of the note or rest it follows.
*Example: a half note has **2 beats**; a dotted half note has 2 + 1 = **3 beats**.*

VALUES OF NOTES AND RESTS

𝅝 ▬ **4 beats**	𝅝. ▬. **6 beats (4+2)**	𝅘𝅥 𝄽 **1 beat**	𝅘𝅥. 𝄽. **1½ beats (1+½)**
𝅗𝅥 ▬ **2 beats**	𝅗𝅥. ▬. **3 beats (2+1)**	𝅘𝅥𝅮 𝄾 **1/2 beat**	𝅘𝅥𝅮. 𝄾. **3/4 beats (½+¼)**

E Learn to sing or play the song "Our Little Castle." Circle the dotted quarter notes in green and the dotted half notes in yellow.

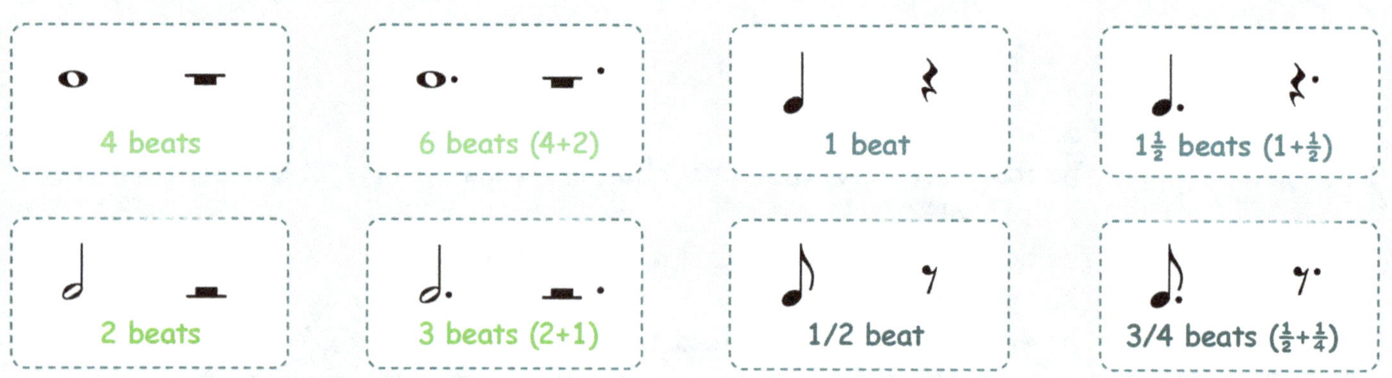

E Draw the notes and rests based on the number of beats specified in the squares. Be mindful of the positioning of the dots following the notes and rests.

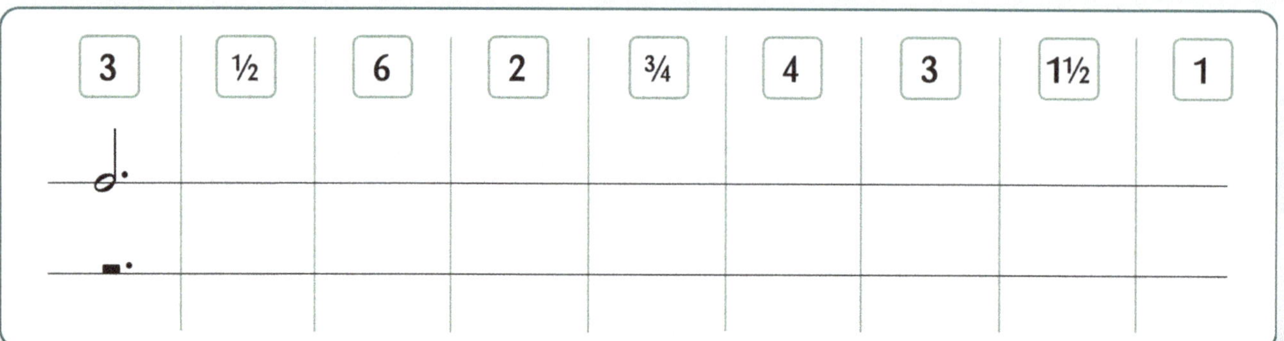

Rhythm, Measure

E Many folk songs contain folk dance rhythmic patterns. Czech folk songs are no exception. A beautiful example of a folk dance is the so-called "baffler," which combines 2/4 and 3/4 rhythms. Learn the song about a pompous rich man representing this particular dance, alternating 2/4 and 3/4 meters, and mark the downbeats.

Clefi & Notelina's Songbook, pg. 58

E Complete each example by indicating the correct time signature.

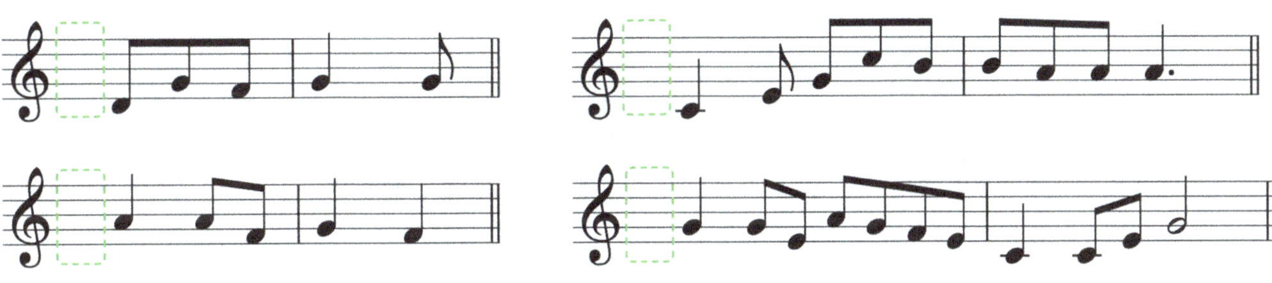

Dynamics

E Organize the following dynamic symbols from the softest to the loudest:
f, mf, mp, p, ff, pp.

- -

Music Vocabulary & Musical Symbols

E Link the symbols to their corresponding terms.

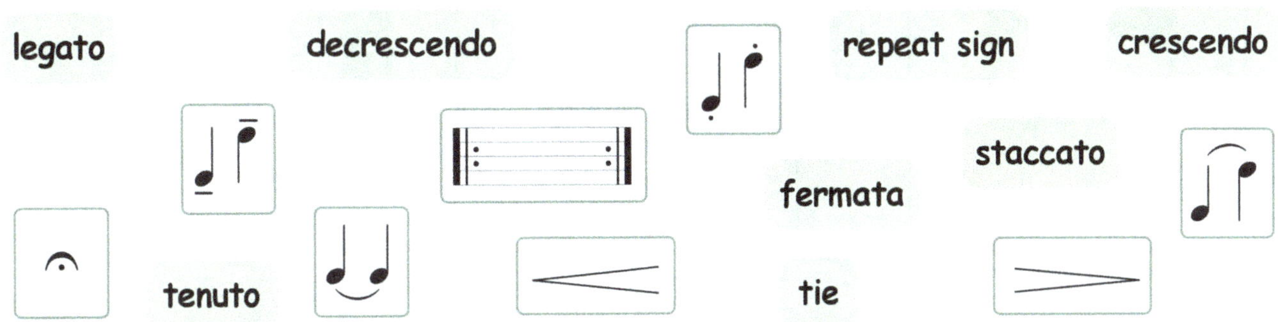

LOWERED TONES

Tones are divided into **primary and altered.**
- **Primary** tones are C, D, E, F, G, A, B.
- **Altered tones** are derived from the primary tones by **raising or lowering their pitch.**

LOWERED TONES

A **lowered tone** has a lower pitch than its primary source. When we lower a primary tone by a half-step, we name it by adding the musical symbol "♭" for flats or its name's suffix - "**FLAT**" - after the altered primary tone's name - "B flat."

The names of the altered lowered tones:
C♭ or C flat, D♭ or D flat, E♭ or E flat, F♭ or F flat, G♭ or G flat, A♭ or A flat, and B♭ or B flat.

To play an altered tone lowered by a half-step on a keyboard,
we play the key closest to the primary tone we alter to the left, either black or white.

PRIMARY AND ALTERED TONES

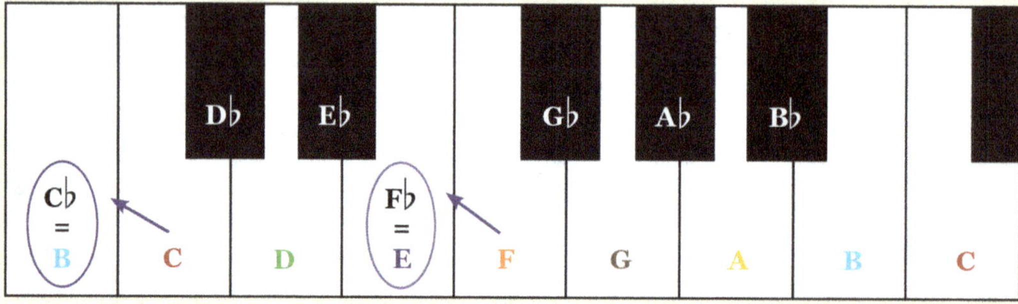

There are no black keys next to the notes **F** and **C**. The altered lowered tones **F♭** and **C♭** don't have their black keys. When we lower **F** or **C** we must play the **white keys closest to them to the left.** The tone **F♭** is played on the primary tone **E** key and the **C♭** on the primary tone **B** key.

E Write the name of the lowered altered tones on the black keys.
Write the names of the keys we use to play tones F flat and C flat.

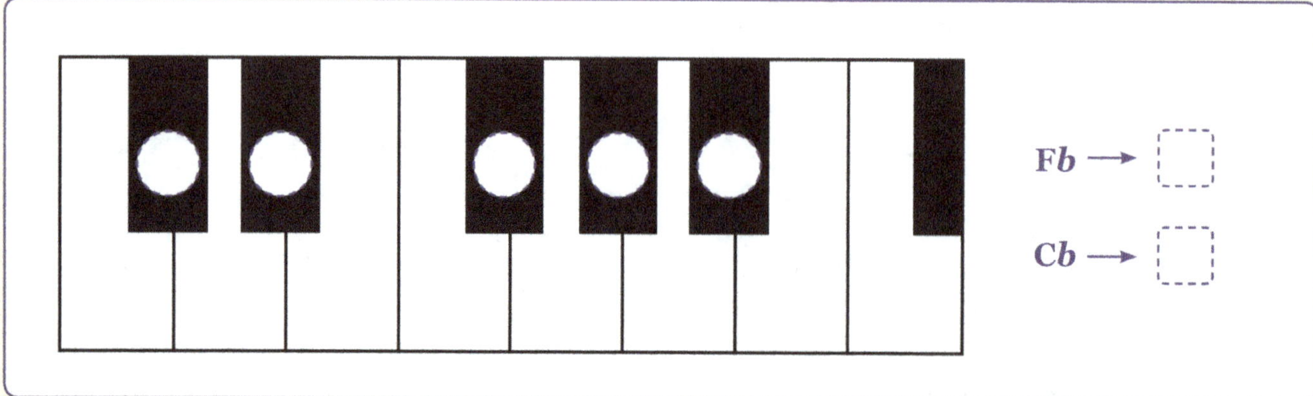

FLATS

A **flat** is an accidental that **lowers** the note's pitch by a **half-step**. If we wish to lower the pitch of a note by a half-step, we have to place the flat right before it. The lowered pitch is then applied to all notes of the same pitch within the measure.

Flats must play by the **same rules** as all other accidentals.
- An accidental must be placed **before the note**.
- The **placement** is very important. An accidental must be placed on the staff exactly as the note it alters.
- An accidental is valid **for the duration of the measure** for the notes of the same pitch in any octave.
- To cancel a sharp or a flat before the measure ends, we use a **natural**.

ALTERED TONES (using flats)

E Draw flats according to the example.

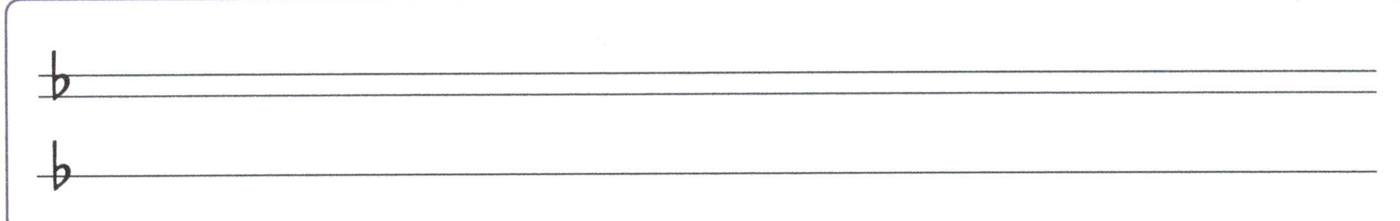

E Write the name of the lowered altered tones from Cb 4 to Cb 5.

E Write the name of the notes into the squares below them.

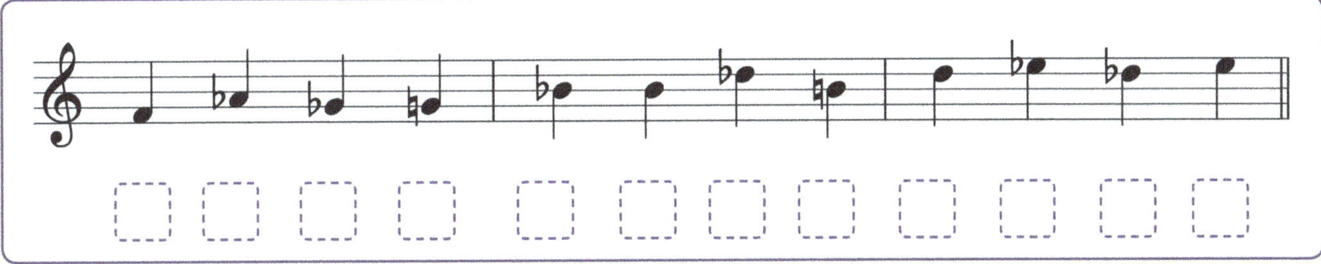

37

MAJOR SCALES WITH FLATS

The C major scale is the primary major scale, it has no sharps and no flats.
In addition to the C major scale, there are **7 scales with sharps** and **7 with flats**.

The major scales with lowered tones - altered using flats - **are the major scales with flats**.

MAJOR SCALES WITH FLATS
F major, Bb major, Eb major, Ab major, Db major, Gb major, Cb major

- Major scales with flats progress either on the **lower P5s** or their inversions **upper P4s**. We will focus on the ascending progression.
- The primary major scale is **C major**, which has **no key signature**.
- Each subsequent major scale with flats begins on the **lower P5** or **upper P4** of the previous scale.
- With each new scale, an additional **flat** is introduced on **its fourth degree**.
- The flats are added in this specific order: **Bb, Eb, Ab, Db, Gb, Cb, and Fb.**

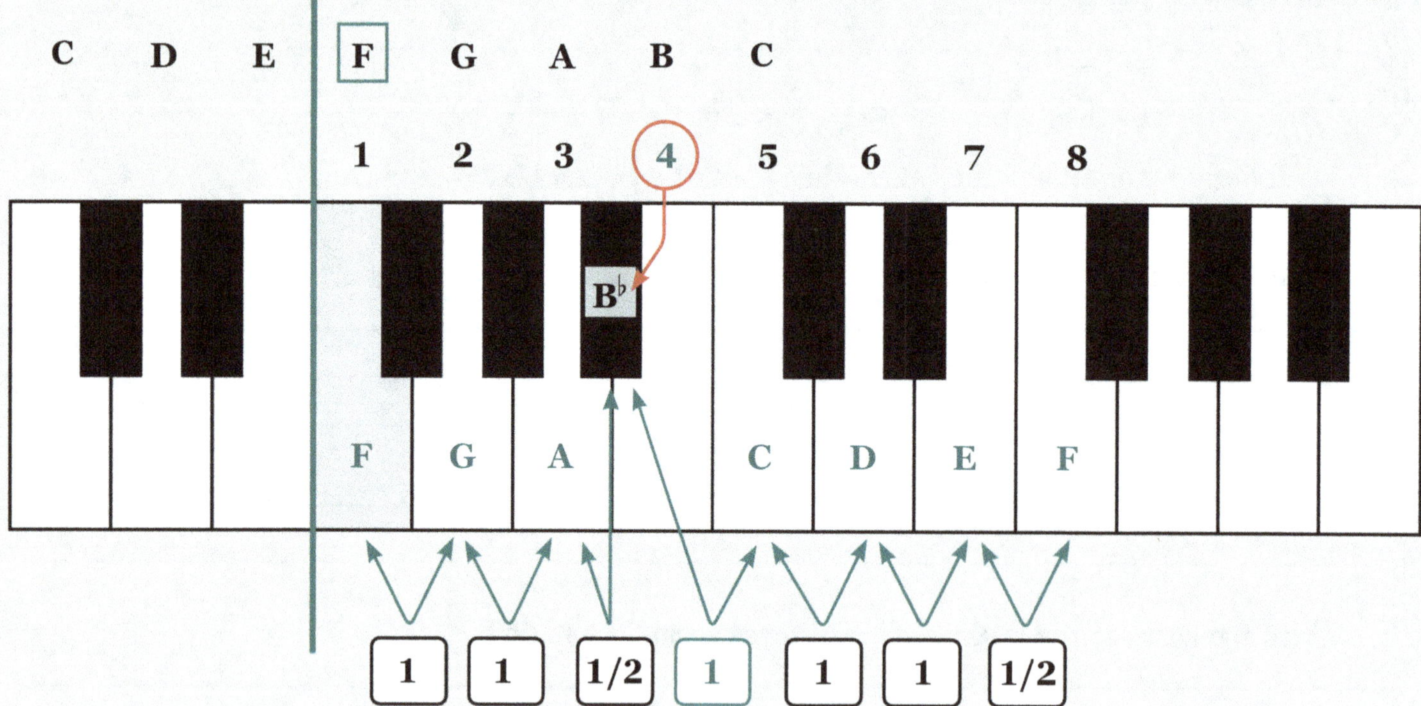

Let's test what we learned by building the first major scale with flats.
(Use the staff paper at the end of the book).

- *We start with the primary major scale, the C major scale (no accidentals).*
- *The scale with one flat starts on the lower fifth or upper fourth degree of the C major scale - the tone F.*
- *F is the root tone of the next scale. We should end up building the **F major** scale.*
- *We start by writing down the row of primary tones starting from F up: **F-G-A-B-C-D-E-F.***
- *To preserve the structure of a major scale - **1-1-1/2-1-1-1-1/2** - we must lower the new scale's fourth step using a flat - **B to Bb.***
- *The tones of the new scale are F, G, A, Bb, C, D, E, F - **F major**, with **one flat**, Bb.*

The **time signature** is always right after the clef on every staff of the piece. Flats are added in the following order: B*b*, E*b*, A*b*, D*b*, G*b*, C*b*, and F*b*.

The **Circle of Fifth** with the major scales with flats.

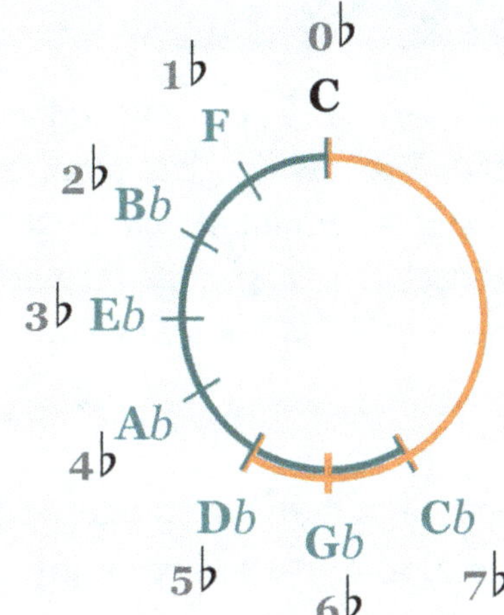

E Write the flats on the staff in the correct order, then write their names on the dotted line below.

E Examine the notation of the F major scale. Write the names of the notes into the squares below them. Use a red pencil to indicate the half-steps and blue to define the tetrachords.

E Learn the song "Hey, You Band of Music Makers." Find and circle all the lowered tones.

Clefi & Notelina's Songbook, pg. 60

TONE "H" OR "B" OR...?

In numerous European countries, sharps and flats alter the name of the note. Sharps take on the suffix "-is," while flats use "-es." For instance, C# becomes Cis, and Db turns into Des. However, there's an intriguing exception: the note "H." This note corresponds to our "B." When the note "H" is lowered, it transforms into either "Hes" or simply "B." Not "B flat," simply "B." Their "B" is our "B flat," while our "B" is their "H." Mind boggling, right? So, what's the origin of this fascinating mystery?

Mystery of Tones "H" and "B"

Long time ago, when people first began to express themselves through song, they created a variety of melodies to express joy, sorrow, or the blues. As creativity flourished, they incorporated rhythmic elements, tapping and clinking on any surface that could produce a beat. Thus, musical instruments were born. In no time, percussion instruments were complemented by flutes and stringed instruments. Among the earliest stringed instruments were the lyre, lute, and harp. The harp soon became a very popular instrument in royal society. It was an instrument that not only accompanied the music but on which people could play the entire song just as they sang it.

After a while, musicians creating melodies started to wonder, "Why not capture tunes like artworks?" But they ran into a problem – there was no established method for music notation. And so those innovative musicians began labeling harp strings with letters, starting with A, much like the alphabet. These labels corresponded to the sequence we recognize from the white keys on a keyboard, but beginning with A: A, B, C, D, E, F, G. This sequence then repeated at various registers, mirroring the layout of later invented keyboard instruments.

Now, if everyone could sing comfortably using the tones of the established tone row - A, B, C, D, E, F, G - all would be great. However, due to people's different voice ranges, the melodies had to be properly adjusted - transposed. This is where the transformative key change comes into play, moving the melody by a couple of steps. However, to maintain the established tone row structure with its half-steps and whole steps, one courageous note had to be altered - lowered. And the note was the note "B." So, the harp player had to down-tune the original B a half-step lower. But they had to find a name for this altered tone.

Musicians embraced their creativity by designating a square-looking B for the original note B and a small round shape b for its lowered sibling. Nevertheless, this led to widespread confusion and numerous mix-ups! To resolve the issue, musical experts renamed the square "B" as "H," which not only resembled the square "B" but also followed next in the alphabet. And just like that, the original note was renamed "H" and the lowered tone kept the original name "B."

CERTIFICATE

OF COMPLETION

This certificate is presented to:

For successfully completing

Clefi's Music Notebook 1

music education teacher

Clefi's and Notelina's
Little American-British Music Dictionary

Music is a universal language; that is true. However, every nation uses its own beautiful tongue to describe and teach music. Clefi is originally Klíček, a little Czech boy who guides children through the fundamentals of music theory using the Czech language and music terminology. His American twin brother Clefi had to translate and adapt the text so English-speaking children could enjoy the journey. However, not all English-speaking musicians use the same music terms. Therefore, Clefi created this little American-British Music Dictionary of music terms used in this book to accommodate our British English-speaking music friends.

Octaves

Zero octave .... Sub-contra octave

First octave .... Contra octave

Second octave .... Great octave

Thirds octave .... Small octave

Fourth (middle) octave .... One-line octave

Fifth octave .... Two-line octave

Sixth octave .... Three-line octave

Seventh octave .... Four-line octave

Notes

C1-B1 .... C, (contra) - B, (contra)

C2-B2 .... C (great) - B (great)

C3-B3 .... c (small) - b (small)

C4-B4 (middle) .... c'-b' (one-line c - 1 line b)

C5-B5 .... c''-b'' (two-line c - 2 line b)

C6-B6 .... c'''-b''' (three-line c - 3 line b)

C7-B7 .... Cc''''-b'''' (four-line c - 4 line b)

General Music Terms

Staff (Staffs) .... Stave (Staves)

Grand staff .... Great stave

Measure, measure line .... Bar, Barline

Fermata .... Pause, Hold

Note Distances

Whole step .... Tone

Half step .... Semitone

Note Values

Double whole note (rest) .... Breve (rest)

Whole note (rest) .... Semibreve (rest)

Half note (rest) .... Minim (rest)

Quarter note (rest) .... Crotchet (rest)

Eighth note (rest) .... Quaver (rest)

Sixteenth note (rest) .... Semiquaver (rest)

Thirty-second note .... Demisemiquaver

(rest)   (rest)

Sixty-fourth note .... Hemidemisemiquaver

(rest)   (rest)

Answer Key to Clefi's Little Crossword Review

Down:

1. G clef.
2. The musical symbols for silence in music.
3. The musical symbol for the soft sound.
4. The meaning of the letter C used instead of its numeric time signature alternative.
6. An example of an ordinary sound in nature.
7. A melodic musical sound.
8. Small sections of musical notation helping organize it.
13. The parts of a musical staff.
17. The short lines helping with the placement of notes outside of the staff.
18. The difference between C and D.
19. F clef.
23 The pulse of a musical piece.

Across:

5. The musical grid used to notate music.
9. The scale built from the primary tone row.
10. The musical symbol for the loud sound.
11. A part of the notes shorter than a whole note.
12. A musical piece past through generations by singing.
14. CDEFGAB.
15. A musical instrument playing rhythmical musical sounds.
16. Parts of notes shorter than a quarter note.
20. Short vertical lines separating measures.
21. Smallest difference between two notes.
22. The sense that helps us identify sounds.
24. The time signature.

Clefi's and Notelina's Little Music Vocabulary

Music is indeed a universal language. However, when explaining the musical terms and commands related to interpreting a piece in musical notation, one language takes center stage. You you have learned a few terms using it in this book. Do you remember how we say "gradually louder" and "gradually softer" in the language of music? That's right! It's "crescendo" (kruh-shen-dow) and "decrescendo" (dee-kruh-shen-dow). Most musical terms are in Italian, and as musicians, we must embrace and utilize them. Now, we will learn some more. So, *Andiamo!*

	DYNAMICS	
pianississimo	ppp	as softly as possible
pianissimo	pp	very softly
piano	p	softly
mezzo piano	mp	moderately softly
mezzo forte	mf	moderately loudly
forte	f	loudly
fortissimo	ff	very loudly
fortississimo	fff	as loudly as possible
crescendo	**cresc.** $<$	gradually louder
decrescendo	**decresc.** $>$	gradually softer
	TEMPOS	
adagio	**66-76 Beats Per Minute**	slowly
andante	**76-108 BPM**	walking pace
moderato	**108-120 BPM**	moderately
allegro	**120-168 BPM**	happily, fast
presto	**168-200 BPM**	very fast
ritardando	**rit., ritard.**	gradually slower
accelerando	**accel.**	gradually faster

Join Clefi's musical family!

Clefi invites you to visit his dedicated webpage and explore the enchanting musical world of Dr. Eva's New Music Education School Series. Learn more about the author and about the content of every volume of the series, dive into engaging materials, find answers to all the exercises, discover more songs, and further deepen your love and understanding of music and music education. Come make music with us!

www.bumblebeenotes.com/clefis-musical-world

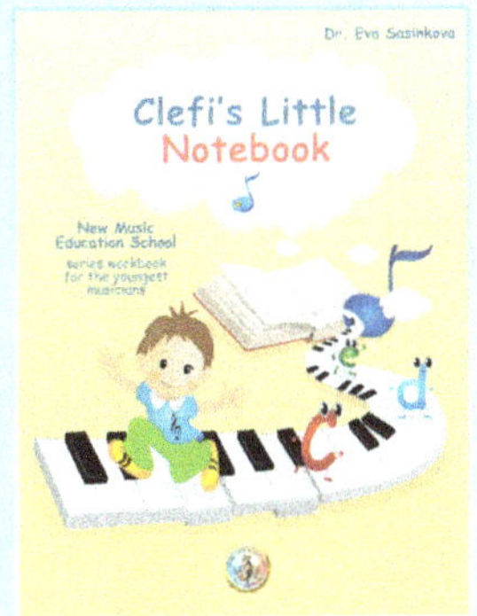

www.bumblebeenotes.com/music-publishing